The Seasons

We would like to express our appreciation to
Mr. Alfred Olivetti,
the Dino Olivetti Foundation,
and the Departments of Italian and Classics
at the College of Charleston, Charleston, South Carolina.

Studi & Testi 4

directed by

LUIGI MONGA & DINO S. CERVIGNI

A COLLECTION OF MONOGRAPHS OF
ANNALI D'ITALIANISTICA
THE UNIVERSITY OF NORTH CAROLINA AT CHAPEL HILL
CHAPEL HILL, NC 27599-3170

GIUSEPPE CONTE

The Seasons

Edited and translated
from the Italian
by
Laura Stortoni-Hager

Introduction
by
Diane di Prima

Afterward
by
Massimo Maggiari

Annali d'italianistica, Inc.
Chapel Hill, NC 27599-3170

Original Title: *Le stagioni*. Milano: Rizzoli, © Copyright 1988

English translation © Copyright 2001
Annali d'italianistica, Inc.
All rights reserved
Manufactured in the United States of America

AdI, Studi & Testi 4
A collection of monographs sponsored by
Annali d'italianistica, Inc.
and directed by Luigi Monga & Dino S. Cervigni.
The University of North Carolina at Chapel Hill
Chapel Hill, NC 27599-3170

Library of Congress Control Number: 2001086991

GIUSEPPE CONTE
THE SEASONS
1.   Poetry: Italian & English.
2.   Italian literature.
ISBN 0-9657956-3-2

The Seasons
$21.
Annali d'italianistica, Inc.
Chapel Hill, NC 27599-3170
Fax: (919) 962 5457
e-mail: annali@metalab.unc.edu
www.ibiblio.org/annali

CONTENTS

PART II

LE STAGIONI DELL'ACQUA / THE SEASONS OF THE WATER

LE STAGIONI DELLA TERRA / THE SEASONS OF THE EARTH

LE STAGIONI DELL'ARIA / THE SEASONS OF THE AIR

LE STAGIONI DEL FUOCO / THE SEASONS OF THE FIRE

DOPO LE STAGIONI / AFTER THE SEASONS

BIOGRAPHICAL INFORMATION ON GIUSEPPE CONTE

A complex and many-faceted individual, Giuseppe Conte is regarded as one of the most important figures in Italian contemporary literature and is well-known as a poet, novelist, playwright and literary critic.

Born in Imperia, Liguria, in 1945, Giuseppe Conte studied at the Università Statale of Milan, earning a degree in literature in 1968 with a thesis on aesthetics. Conte edited the review *Il Verri* and has contributed literary theory and criticism essays to numerous reviews and journals, such as *Nuova corrente*, *Sigma*, *Altri termini*, *L'altro versante*, and *Tema celeste*. After leaving the teaching profession, Conte became poetry editor for the publisher Guanda. He writes for newspapers such as *Stampa sera*, *Il giornale*, and *Mercurio* (cultural supplement of *La repubblica*). Conte recently produced and hosted a special poetry feature series for Italian public television station RAI 2.

Conte's first book of criticism, *La metafora barocca* (*Baroque Metaphor*), was published in 1972. He has subsequently written on the rhetorics of baroque aesthetics and literary criticism of such writers as Aldo Palazzeschi, Aubrey Beardsley, and D. H. Lawrence. His early works of poetry, as well as his theoretical essays, have made him a leading figure in the movement for the renewal of Italian poetry. Conte inaugurated the idea of poetry as dance, desire, passion, and energy beyond experimentalism and ideological engagement. His poetic writings center around the great themes of myth and nature, and find expression in his book *L'ultimo aprile bianco* (*The Last White April*, 1979), which had a tremendous impact on Italian poetry, and *L'oceano e il ragazzo* (*The Ocean and the Boy*, 1983), which garnered the acclaim of authors such as Italo Calvino and Pietro Citati. *L'oceano e il ragazzo* was translated into French by Jean-Baptiste Para and won the Nelly Sachs Prize for the best poetry translation in 1989. With his book of poetry, *Le stagioni* (*The Seasons*, 1988), Conte won the coveted Montale Prize, while *Il dialogo del poeta e del messaggero* (*Dialogue between Poet and Messenger*, 1992) had a second edition only a few months after the initial publication. The latter collection includes the poetry suite *"Democrazia"* (*Democracy*), which touches on themes and tones of civil poetry, introducing a Whitmanesque style new to Italy. His most recent poetry volume, entitled *Canti d'oriente e d'occidente* (*Songs of the East and the West*) appeared in May 1997.

Conte published his first novel, *Primavera incendiata* (*Burned Spring*), in 1980, followed by four other novels: *Equinozio d'autunno*

(*Autumn Equinox*, 1987*)*, *I giorni della nuvola* (*Days of the Cloud*, 1990), *Fedeli d'amore* (*Love's Faithful*, 1993), and *L'impero e l'incanto* (*The Empire and the Enchantment*, 1995), which was on the Italian bestseller list. In addition, Conte published a book of essays on travel and myth, *Terre del mito* (*Lands of myth*, 1991), which has also been published in a French translation. He also published a dual-language edition of the diary from his first sojourn in Brittany, *Le Manuscript de Saint-Nazaire* (*The Manuscript of St. Nazaire*, 1989), several books of criticism, including *Il mito giardino* (*The Garden Myth*, 1990), and a poetry manual. His most recent novel is *Il ragazzo che parla col sole* (*The Boy who Speaks with the* Sun, Milano: Longanesi, 1998).

A lover of music and theater, Conte has written two opera librettos, collaborating with musician Gianni Possio and artist Mimmo Paladino. For the first festival of the *Mitomodernismo* movement at Alassio in the summer of 1995, Conte created *L'Iliade e il jazz* (*The Iliad and Jazz*), a poetic opera in collaboration with bass player Dodo Goya. Summoned to Brittany by the Maison des écrivains de théatre étrangers, Conte wrote the comedy *Re Artù e i senzatetto / Le Roy Arthur et les sans-logis* (*King Arthur and the Homeless*, 1995), a dual-language work staged at Saint-Herblain, France, and Turin, Italy. In 1981, Conte authored an anthology on metaphor, and in 1990, published a monumental anthology, *La lirica d'occidente* (*Western Lyric Poetry*, 1990), comprising texts from the Homeric hymns to contemporary poetry. Conte has translated Blake, Shelley, Whitman and Lawrence, whom he regards as the primary inspirations of his own personal poetry, in addition to Goethe, Foscolo, and twentieth-century Ligurian poets. He is deeply interested in contemporary American poetry and Native American history and spirituality. Dubbed a "great traveler" by *Le Monde*, Conte has been traveling for years for poetry readings, lectures, or simply for the pleasure of following his own myths, from Morocco to Indonesia, from Ireland to India. He has read his poetry in France, Germany, Great Britain, Spain, Switzerland, Holland, Greece, Sweden, Russia, Algeria, South Africa, Colombia, Canada, Venezuela, Argentina and the United States, in particular in the Bay Area, upon invitation of the San Francisco Italian Cultural Institute in 1992.

On October 1, 1994, Conte staged a peaceful occupation of the Church of Santa Croce in Florence with a group of poets, and, after the ritual reading of Foscolo's *I sepolcri* in front of the poet's tomb, launched his message for the spiritual renewal of poetry.

In January 1995, in Milan, Conte founded the *Mitomodernismo* movement, whose goals are the return of myth to art and the embodying of mythical archetypes in contemporary reality. In 1996, he was called by UNESCO to participate in an international scientific committee for the creation of the World Institute for Opera and Poetry in Verona.

The Ocean and the Boy, Conte's first full-length book of poetry to be translated into English, appeared in a dual-language edition in 1997 (Berkeley: Hesperia Press). This volume of poetry, *The Seasons,* is the second complete book of Conte's poetry to appear in the United States.

He lives in Porto Maurizio, Liguria, and in Nice, France.

INTRODUCTION

BY DIANE DI PRIMA

The Archetype of the Poet—who or what s/he is—is an endangered one as we begin this new Millennium. The true Poet, that is, not the literary careerist, or the emotional solipsist, or the academician, or even the political revolutionary.

The Poet has no mission but poetry, no ambition but obedience to the Art, no country but the World, and this includes not only our beloved planet, but the Stars beyond. S/he must, as Pico said of the Magician, "marry the World." For at this time in our history, we have no Magicians, no Priests, but our artists—and they, as I have said, are few and far between.

To "marry the World": This includes the world of Time as well as Space: "All ages are contemporaneous within the mind," as Ezra Pound said. Needless to say, the world of time includes the Timeless, as space includes the Boundless.

The Poet walks in Atlantis, sings with Sappho, sails with the Hopi from the lost Third World of Lemuria to the Western edge of what we now call the Americas. S/he speaks the lost languages of tribes long passed from the earth, worships in the Religions of Light which still dwell and glimmer, barely seen beneath the dull orthodoxies which keep the human species bound and afraid.

The Poet is a devotee of the Religions of Light, which are the Religions of Love, and speaks a language not yet born ... for in the realms of Art it is the future as well as the past that is "contemporaneous."

Giuseppe Conte is a Poet in this full sense, and as such he is a National—no, an International, a Worldwide—Treasure. His work is ageless. Because he does not seek poetry for his own ends, his relation to the world—to sea and sky, to gods and humans—is pristine and his voice is untrammeled. It is pure Song that we find on these pages, as it was in Sumer, and Greece, and Provence, and will be again in the times to come.

Laura Stortoni-Hager's translation holds true to Conte's work, both his meaning and intent. Her work is fluid and eloquent, with the transparency so necessary to a good translation. Her knowledge of this body of work (she also translated and published Conte's first book of poetry) makes the poems' translation seem effortless.

But do not be deceived: This is no "easy" poetry; its seamless workmanship is the result of a vast erudition. Conte is casual; he is formal. He tells us almost everything; he tells us nothing. His is a poetry of surfaces; of depths. He shows us the Poet: it is the transparent-pink newborn gecko in your mailbox, the brash, ungainly Scotch broom bursting with light, that will uproot our highways. The Poet is present at the death of Pan, and also knows that death to be a lie.

See how the light shifts and changes as Conte changes the filter on his lens. The seasons slide over the world of the gods, of the animals, of plants, of humans. The Seasons of Venus are not the Seasons of Hermes, he shows us. Each cycle discrete, shining. Separable. All these worlds, one.

Paracelsus once said that the element that predominates in any one thing, at any time, can be identified, not by its substance, but by its dynamics of change. In Part II of the present work, Conte reveals a part of that dynamic: an infinitesimal, profound, cross-section of the Dance of the Elements. Look with care: there is more than Language at work here.

Paracelsus also tells us: "To conjure is nothing more than to see rightly." To recognize. Giuseppe is a conjurer.

EDITOR-TRANSLATOR' S NOTE

I first came across Conte's poetry in 1988 during one my summer trips to Milan to see my family and to catch up with the Italian literary scene. I bought *L'oceano e il ragazzo* at my favorite bookstore under the Galleria. I started reading it on the subway home, and became so engrossed that I missed my stop. After my return to the Unites States, I translated several poems so that I could share them with my friends and students, and published a few in reviews and journals, such as *The Midwest Quarterly*, *The New Renaissance*, and *The Barnabe Mountain Review*. Charles Simic says that "the translator is like the one who wants to disseminate the Gospels." I wanted to share the revelations I had found in Conte's poetry.

I have just published *The Ocean and the Boy* (Berkeley: Hesperia Press, 1997) in dual-language edition, and I now present Conte's second book of poetry, *The Seasons*, which won the coveted Montale Prize the year it was published, 1988.

The word *translation*, from the Latin *transferre*, means essentially to carry something from one place to another. The literary translator carries words—the heaviest of loads—from one language to another. But the very act of choosing one poet above another is firstly an act of identification. A special chord is struck, for remote and arcane reasons, allowing the translator no peace until the original poetry is fully digested, absorbed and regurgitated in the other language, having become the translator's flesh and fiber. My wish to translate Conte's poetry stemmed from my own deep identification with his themes and style.

The first draft of these translations was ready for Conte's lectures and readings in the Bay Area in 1992, to be read after the Italian texts. Throughout the years, these translations have been revised with care.

Conte's style is not easy to translate. He often uses syntactical and grammatical constructions of his own creation impossible to render in English. His vocabulary, reflecting an enormous and varied knowledge, is extraordinarily rich. His style is simple but accurate, laden with culture without being pedantic. His precision in naming and describing plants and flowers sent me several times to the Berkeley Botanical Gardens. Conte describes animals and flowers with an attention to detail reminiscent of the poetry of D. H. Lawrence, a poet he dearly loves. Words, adjectives, clauses, sentences, come to Conte in rapid succession, at times without punctuation, dictated by the *daimon* within. Since English is syntactically simpler than Italian, it was at times necessary to introduce punctuation where there was none in the original, so that its meaning would not be lost. Lost in English were, unfortunately, some of the many inversions Conte uses to leave the Italian reader with a sense of suspension. At times, sentences with many clauses had to be broken down to suit modern English usage.

Conte's poetry is inspired, bursting out in sudden images and metaphors in a "high style" that has caused him to be occasionally likened to D'Annunzio. Yet, the "high style" is often created with the simplest of words, the plainest of expressions. Such is the stuff of myth, the stuff of Conte's poetry: magic worked and achieved through the most elemental of means.

In my translation, I strive to keep as close as possible to the original text, so that my translation may serve as an arrow pointing in the direction of the original text. I attempted to make the lines of the Italian and English texts coincide, but I broke this self-imposed rule a few times, whenever it was necessary for the rhythm of the English poem. Musicality is such an essential component of Conte's poetry that it was more important to reproduce the rhythm of the original than to slavishly adhere to a line count. Conte, a well-known and inspired literary translator, knows that capturing the essence of a poem in a foreign language is more important than following it word by word: a translated poem should read like a poem. But, no matter how hard the translator tries, he/she presents the reverse side of the tapestry, showing the pattern, but lacking some of the brilliance and the texture of the original weave.

Translating Conte was for me either spontaneous, almost automatic for some poems, or, for others, a laborious process sending my fingers flying through numerous dictionaries, mythology manuals and reference books. I had, however, the luxury of being able to contact the author by phone or fax, a luxury I did not have while translating Renaissance texts.

Conte's poetry, like Conte the individual, is either extremely simple, or extremely complex. This collection is possibly the most erudite of Conte's five books of poetry; therefore, I felt that the endnotes were essential, especially since many poems are replete with scholarly allusions and references to the legends and the archetypes of the classical world, with which the American reader may not be familiar. For the explanatory notes, I am indebted to Conte himself, as well as to Giorgio Ficara, who wrote the footnotes for the original volume that guided me in the writing of my own endnotes.

Having had the honor of meeting Conte, and having become friends with him, I see him as he sees himself: essentially a wanderer, traveling from city to city, from country to country, in the quest for the Word, or for the experience or emotion generating from the utterance of the Word.

The themes of this book are, *in nuce*, literature and myth, childhood and poetry. The nature presented in this book is rich in myth, and the poet's style is as varied as the nature he describes with such loving detail. Conte is not a follower of the "hermetic" tradition, nor is he a "modernista." His style is intensely personal, produced by a unique fusion of myths and beliefs from disparate civilizations, from classical Greece and Rome, to Nordic myth, to American Indian and Aztec mythology: subjects Conte explores later in detail in *Terre del mito* (*Lands of Myth*). His is the simplest, and yet the most sumptuous of styles, and his culture-laden poetry also has the directness of a child's word. His native Celtic Liguria ties the poet to Ireland and to Nordic mythologies. But his Mediterranean origins (his father was Sicilian) also tie him to Greece, giving his poetry the dark intensity of the deep Mediterranean and a natural identification with the islands and the classical sites.

Conte's dry Ligurian landscape appearing in many of his poems has placed him in the illustrious line of Ligurian poets, from Montale to Sbarbaro. Calvino saw Conte as a poet devoted to Diana, the Goddess; and yet, Conte is also rooted in the humble reality of the two slate steps of his childhood in Porto Maurizio, to the peeling facades of the house in the street where he was born. He is a wanderer aware of life's cyclic succession, traveling to return, full circle, to his starting point.

Conte has visited the United States several times, and was in the Bay Area for an extended visit in the Fall of 1992, when he came at the invitation of the San Francisco Cultural Institute. He read at the Italian Cultural Institute, lectured for the Comparative Literature Department at the University of California at Berkeley and read poetry at the Casa Italiana, was a guest of the San Francisco Poetry Center, and gave a memorable reading at the Marin Poetry Center in San Rafael. He met with many local poets, among whom Lawrence Ferlinghetti, Diane di Prima, and Czeslaw Milosz. After a reading, a student who had never written poetry wrote to tell me she had been so inspired by Conte's poetry that she had gone home to write her first poem!

Conte is very interested in modern American poetry, and is particularly fond of Native American mythology, which he personally explored during a trip to the South West, a literary pilgrimage to recapture D. H. Lawrence's spirit. He has a photograph of Geronimo on the wall of his study, and for years one of his favorite books has been *Bury My Heart at Wounded Knee*. From Native American culture he has taken, he says, the deep sense of identification with nature that permeates his poetry.

I have also translated most of Conte's *Dialogo del poeta e del messaggero* (*Dialogue between the Poet and the Messenger*), and I plan to prepare a volume of his selected poems in the future. I hope that the reader will share my enthusiasm for this poet who has affected me deeply. For me, translating is like opening a door to others, to welcome them in, to show them the treasures I have found in another space, in another language. My task, as a translator, is to offer what would otherwise be unavailable, to give, in Conte's words,

the immense, light gift
of the poem

Berkeley, January 2001

PARTE PRIMA

LE STAGIONI DI VENERE

PART I

THE SEASONS OF VENUS

Come saranno al largo le stagioni?
Lo sai tu che hai passato
i mari per cercare la tua isola.
Si conoscono le primavere
forse dai mandorli, dai meli
improvvisi di onde e vento,
da tiepide correnti straniere,
da migranti meduse.

D'estate l'orizzonte è un miraggio
come quel lago salato
dove sostavano i cavalli
da tiro, come un ibisco incrostato
di polvere ai bordi di una strada
di Cipro.

Si dice che d'autunno i boschi
opachi e casti dei fondali si spogliano:
si disfano i pioppi tremuli
di laggiù, silenziosi vortici.

E negli inverni il mare è cancellato
come giardini da troppa neve.
Tu dove sei?
Resta soltanto il corso obliquo e breve
del Sole, e il mondo rado delle ombre.

How will the seasons be out at sea?
You know, you who have crossed
the seas to look for your island.
One perhaps knows the spring
from the almond and the apple trees
suddenly quivering with waves and winds,
from the warm foreign currents,
from the migrant jellyfish.

In the summer the horizon is a mirage,
like the salty lake
where the draught horses used to rest,
like a hibiscus encrusted with dust
at the edges of a street
in Cyprus.

They say that in autumn the opaque,
chaste woods at the bottom of the sea
shed their leaves: the trembling poplars fall apart
down there, like silent vortexes.

And in the winter the sea is erased
like gardens covered by too much snow.
And you, where are you?
There remains only the brief, oblique course
of the Sun, and the rarefied world of the shadows.

INVERNO

Ades

Se la neve fa gli alberi di cenere
quando il buio precipita, se il mare
è sbiadito di nebbie, irriconoscibile
e cercano gli alati un riparo
sotto la siepe smagrita, o dove
la sabbia della spiaggia finge un tepore
contro i maestrali

quando il gelo fa friabili le foglie
sopravvissute, e baca sullo stelo
l'ultimo fiore del geranio
e sul sentiero bianco più che di sale
le tue orme ti seguono

non voltarti: è il mondo delle ombre
il mio inverno,
il regno rado, eterno
della non-esistenza, il confine della luce.
Non voltarti: c'è un frutto, c'è un ricordo[1]
il cui sapore sempre riconduce
quaggiù.

---

[1] *c'è un frutto...*: secondo il mito, Proserpina, durante il suo soggiorno nell'Ade, assaggiò la melagrana. Per questo motivo, oltre che per il patto stabilito da Cerere e Ades, ogni inverno dovette tornare negli inferi.

WINTER

Hades

If the snow turns the trees the color of ash
when darkness suddenly falls, if the sea fades,
unrecognizable, beneath the mist,
and the winged creatures seek shelter
under a thinning hedge or where
the sand of the shore feigns a warmth
against the North-West winds

When the frost makes the surviving leaves
crumble, and the last geranium flower
is worm-eaten in its stem,
and on a path whiter than salt
your footprints follow you

Do not look back: it is the world of shadows—
my winter—
the eternal rarefied kingdom
of non-existence, the confines of light.
Do not look back: there is a fruit, a memory,[1]
whose flavor always
leads us back here.

---

[1] According to the myth, after being abducted by Hades, Persephone ate some pomegranate seeds, the food of the dead. For this reason, as well for the agreement between Ceres and the god of the Underworld, Persephone was bound to return to Hades every winter, and divided her time between the underworld and the world of the living.

PRIMAVERA

Proserpina

Così nacque il mondo, di questa
stagione, Madre? Così si schiusero
i vulcani, così scesero
le piogge tiepide a circondare
le terreferme di Oceano?
Guarda come le rose e i ranuncoli
sgorgano sulle siepi e sui
prati, guarda come gli anemoni
insanguinati fanno sentiero
al vento. Calano gli alati
ad amarsi tra i canneti, i cavalli
corrono in riva ai torrenti,
coprono le cavalle.

E io di chi sarò, Madre? Senti
anche tu che questo fiorire vasto e
purpureo è minaccioso
come se dovesse aprire
le bocche l'Etna?

"Portaci madre dei fiori
futuri dall'aspra Eritrea
l'euforbia, e dall'India
la calma, veleggiante magnolia.

Lo sai che cosa il girasole
teme ogni tramonto nel cielo
e il ricordo di quale amore[1]
lo piega sopra lo stelo?

---

[1] *quale amore…*: allusione al mito di Clizia, figlia dell'Oceano e di Teti, che innamorata senza fortuna di Apollo fino al punto di lasciarsi morire, fu tramutata dal dio impietosito nel fiore di girasole.

SPRING

Persephone

Was the world born thus, Mother, in this
season? Did the volcanoes
open up, did the warm rains
fall like this to surround
the *terra firma* with Ocean?
See how the roses and the buttercups
spill over from hedges and from meadows,
see how the bloodied
anemones make a path
for the wind! The winged creatures
come down to make love among the reeds, the horses
run on the river-banks
and mount the mares.

And to whom will I belong, Mother? Do you also
feel that this vast and
purple flowering is menacing,
as if Aetna where about to open
its mouth?[1]

"Mother of future
flowers, bring us the euphorbia
from arid Eritrea, and from India
the calm, sail-like magnolia.

Do you know what the sunflower
fears every time the sun sets in the sky,
or the memory of what love[2]
bends it upon its stem?

---

[1] Aetna: volcano in Sicily. The Tyrrhenian Sea represents the Western part of the Mediterranean.
[2] "The memory of what love": Allusion to the myth of Clytias, daughter of Ocean and Thetis, who loved Apollo, unrequited, to the point of dying. The god, filled with pity, transformed her into a sunflower.

Perché gli anemoni sono
leggeri e rossi come nebulose
perché sono viola le viole
perché sono rosa le rose?

Portaci nuovi colori
qui sulle rive tirrene
stellati di fuoco e che incantano
come al largo le sirene."

Why are anemones light
and red like star-clusters?
Why are violets purple?
Why are roses red?

Bring us new colors
here on the Tyrrhenian shores—
colors starred by fire that can cast
a spell, like the sirens at sea."

ESTATE

Poseidone

Estate tu non declinare.
Resta come sei, maestosa
e oppressiva, tu tiranna
di terraferma.
Porta le meduse sin
sulla sabbia.
Sei tu che hai bordato la rosa
di troppa luce, e pian piano
l'hai disfatta
e tu che alle vigne prometti
il vino lento e dolce.

Mi stendo nelle tue bonacce.

Non declinare.[1] Resta
come sei, nuda e
sola. Amare non è più
necessario.
Tu conosci l'immobilità del piacere.
Porta le meduse sin
sulla sabbia,
decapita i giunchi, incendia
i ginepri. La costa tutte le sere
è come una carcassa bianca.

Sei tu che sospendi nubi
aride sopra le pianure e i carrubi
solitari, sopra le foreste
e le isole
assetate.

Mi stendo nelle tue asciutte
tempeste.

---

[1] *Non declinare*: cfr. D'Annunzio, *Alcyone, Madrigali dell'Estate*: "Estate, Estate mia, non declinare!".

SUMMER

Poseidon[1]

Summer, do not decline.
Stay as your are, majestic
and oppressive, you, tyrant
of *terra firma*.
Bring the jellyfish
as far as the sand.
It's you who adorned the rose
with too much light, you who undid her
little by little,
and it's you who promises to the vineyards
slow and sweet wine.

I stretch out in your dead calm.

Do not decline.[2] Stay
as you are, naked
and alone. To love is no longer
necessary.
You know the immobility of pleasure.
Bring the jellyfish
as far as the sand,
decapitate the reeds, set the junipers
on fire. Every evening the coastline
is like a white carcass.

It's you who hangs arid clouds
over the plains and the solitary
carob-trees, over the forests
and the thirsty
islands.
I stretch out in your dry
tempests.

---

[1] Poseidon: the god of the sea.
[2] See D'Annunzio, *Halcyon, Madrigals of Summer*: "Summer, my summer, do not decline!"

AUTUNNO

Artemide

Nessuno mi avrà. Rimarrò
padrona dei boschi scoscesi
di pini e di pioppi tremuli
delle notti e delle lune.
Manderò cerve a correre
lungo i sentieri sino alla fine.
La catastrofe non mi ferirà
al cuore.
Verrò in città, a mendicare
ai primi freddi, quando
appare l'oro conico di giardini
e chiese ogni tramonto
sosterò sotto i portici, dai ponti
sul fiume scoprirò dove si riposano
i gabbiani che hanno così tanto
viaggiato.
Non mi riconoscerete voi
che andate a casa senza guardare
non saprete mai chi è l'esiliata
ragazza che vi taglia la strada e
ride.

"Dea della castità, delle bacche, delle notti
lunghe, io ti ho invocata"

AUTUMN

Artemis

I will belong to no one. I will remain
mistress of the steep woods,
of pines and poplars
trembling in the nights and the moons.
I will send hinds to run
to the very end of the paths.
I will not let catastrophe
wound my heart.
I will come to the city to beg
at the first frosts, when the golden cones
of the gardens and churches appear
at twilight.
I will linger under the porticoes, from the bridges
on the river I will discover where the seagulls rest
after traveling so far.
You who go home without looking
will not recognize me—
you will never know
who is the exiled girl
cutting in front of you
laughing.

"Goddess of chastity, of wild berries, of long
nights, I have invoked you."

LE STAGIONI DI PAN

THE SEASONS OF PAN[1]

---

[1] In Greek mythology, the god of pastures and flocks. His lower parts were goat-like, and he was fond of music and dancing.

L'ho visto il tramonto sul mare
di Paro. È lento il sole e il cielo
popoloso come un villaggio
mai sconfitto.
Le onde fronteggiano palme
dai tronchi sabbiosi, chiese dalle cupole
azzurre, un mulino.

Il vento guidava veloce
sin quasi alla riva la tavola
dell'ultimo surf. Lontano
si incontravano come due punte di spada
gli scafi dei traghetti
quelli candidi e quelli color
oro.

E ho visto venire la sera
nei boschetti di alloro già neri
e lucidi le cicale ansimare
sopra gli ulivi nani, andare
sperduto un tacchino
tra le stoppie.

E tu, Pan, dov'eri?
Da qui fu annunciata [1]– fu un grido
di tortora o di cratere
acceso? –
la tua morte per tutte le navi
in rotta sull'Egeo
dai porti odorosi di Cipro
a Roma.

---

[1] *Da qui fu annunciata...*: secondo la leggenda, ai tempi dell'imperatore Tiberio, il nostromo di una nave ormeggiata nel porto dell'isola di Paro udì una voce che annunciava la morte di Pan. Nel Medioevo l'episodio divenne emblematico della fine del paganesimo.

I have seen the sunset on the sea
of Paros. The sun is slow and the sky
crowded like an undefeated
village.
The waves face palm-trees
with sandy trunks, churches with blue
domes, a windmill.

The wind was swiftly driving
the last surf-board
almost as far as the shore. Far away,
like the tips of two swords,
the hulls of the ferry-boats met,
some bright white,
some golden.

And I have seen the evening approach
in thickets of laurels already shiny
and blackened, the cicadas panting
upon dwarf olive trees, a turkey
wandering lost
among the stubble.

And you, Pan, where were you?[1]
From here the news of your death (was it the cry
of a dove or the roar of a burning
crater?) spread
throughout all the ships
en route on the Aegean
from the redolent ports of Cyprus
to Rome.

---

[1] *I have seen the sunset on the sea* ....: According to the legend, in the times of Emperor Tiberius, the boatswain of a boat moored in the harbor of the island of Paros (Greek island in the Cyclades) heard a voice announcing the death of Pan. In the Middle Ages, the episode came to symbolize the end of Paganism.

Tornavi? Non era
doma la tua frenesia
zoppa, di farfalla e di
capro, di danzatore
più piagato che osceno, attorto
su di sé, in procinto
di cantare e cadere?

Pan, ti ho riconosciuto
nell'attimo che il silenzio fu
sovrastante: nell'immobilità
esitante del tacchino sperduto,
nelle stoppie arse da una calura
passata: nell'aria rosata che tardava
a divenire scura.

Where you returning? Wasn't your limp
frenzy tamed,
your frenzy of butterfly
and of goat, of dancer
more wounded than obscene, twisted
upon himself, about to
sing and fall?

Pan, I recognized you
in the moment of impending
silence: in the hesitating immobility
of the turkey lost
in the stubble parched by a past
heat wave: in the rosy air that
was slow to darken.

INVERNO

Piazza dei gabbiani

È stato freddissimo, forse
l'inverno più freddo del secolo.
La mano del gelo ha trovato
le buganvillee e i geranei
li ha fatti grigi e friabili
sul muraglione e nelle fioriere.

La neve è caduta anche in riva
al mare; prima di sera
le spiagge chinavano bianche
al lungo confine con le onde:
neve sulle barche rovesciate
a secco, sulle ferriere
abbandonate.

È il freddo che ha fatto volare
i gabbiani sempre più in qua
verso la città, la piazza
centrale.
Il freddo colore del mare
tra Oneglia e Diano, le tempeste,
la poca pesca, non so,
il sole scialbo e lontano,
la fame, la paura.

Il primo che scese e guardò
le tegole rosse e i balconi
dal basso, scoprì
il buio cavo dei portici,
le vetrine, le saracinesche, i marciapiedi.
E altri lo seguirono. Era l'ora
di pranzo. Ne vidi
molti, candidi, indecisi
come soldati assediati in un fortino
muoversi sull'asfalto, vicino
a dove sostano gli autobus

WINTER

The Piazza of the Seagulls

It was bitter cold, maybe
the coldest winter of the century.
The hand of the frost found
the bougainvilleas and the geraniums,
made them gray and crumbly
on the rock wall and in the flower beds.

The snow fell to the edge
of the sea; before evening
the beaches bent low, white,
at the long border with the waves:
snow on the boats turned over
and left to dry, snow on the abandoned
iron works.

The cold made the seagulls fly
this way, closer and closer
to the city, to the central
piazza.
The cold color of the sea
between Oneglia and Diano, the storms,
the scant fishing—who knows?—
the wan and distant sun,
the hunger, the fear.

The first who came down to look
at the red roof-tiles and balconies
from below, discovered
the hollow darkness of the porticoes,
the store windows, the rolling shutters, the sidewalks.
And others followed him. It was
dinner time. I saw many
of them, bright white—undecided,
like soldiers besieged within a fort—
move on the asphalt, near

per Albenga e per la Frontiera.[1]
Non c'era in loro la svelta
sicurezza dei passeri e dei
colombi. Si capiva che erano
stranieri, capitati lì per una
catastrofe più lontana e più vera
del gelo dell'inverno. Uno
alzava un po' le ali, sembravano
gomiti di un ferito, di uno scampato
appena al naufragio.
Altri torcevano a terra
il collo, a beccare forse
rifiuti.

Com'erano imbelli, e quasi
ciechi, e quanto
terrorizzante il loro girovagare
lento lì sulla piazza.

Signori dei flutti, delle lontananze,
come camminavano a stento
sotto una pensilina
e come si vedeva che non sapevano
che fare quando le automobili
li radevano. Non volavano —
alzarsi in volo per loro vuol dire
un poco poter correre, e poi aprire
di colpo ali troppo larghe — restavano
lì al suolo a schivare
le ruote come chi è su piedi
malati, malfermi.

Chi lo sa se volevano morire.
E come gli appariva ancora di là
in basso, in pericolo, il cielo
vasto e chiaro.

---

[1] *la Frontiera*: la frontiera per la Francia.

the bus stop for Albenga and the French border.[1]
The did not have the quick
assurance of the sparrows
and of the pigeons. You could tell
they were aliens who just happened to come here
because of a catastrophe more distant, more real
than the winter frost. One of them
lifted his wings a little, wings that looked like
the elbows of a wounded person, or someone who has just escaped
a shipwreck.
Others on the ground twisted
their necks, maybe to peck
at refuse.

How cowardly they were, and almost
blind, and how
terrifying was their slow wandering
there, on the piazza.

Lords of the waves, of distances,
how slowly they dragged themselves
under a shed,
and how clearly you could see
they did not know what to do
when cars grazed them. They did not fly —
to soar in flight for them
means to be able to run a little,
then to open suddenly wings too wide —
they remained on the ground
to avoid the car wheels like sick people
walking on unsure feet.

Who knows if they wanted to die
and how to them
— still below in danger —
the vast clear sky appeared.

---

[1] Oneglia, Diano and Albenga are cities on the Western Riviera in Liguria, close to where
Conte was born. The poem is reminiscent of the famous albatross poem by Baudelaire
(*Les Fleurs du mal*).

Se lo hanno per un po' rinnegato
e che cosa hanno creduto
che fosse quella piazza di città, chi può
dirlo?

If they disowned it for a while,
and what they thought the city piazza was,
who
can ever tell?

PRIMAVERA

Il geco nella cassetta delle lettere

Ricordi come fu tardi, dopo quasi
due mesi di consultazioni,
che ottenemmo la cassetta delle lettere?
C'era da ridere. I padroni
di casa, anziani, intenti
a tener alto il decoro della
proprietà – i muri imbiancati
di fresco, gli stemmi in alto, la lunga
merlatura, il giardino,
erano incerti, un poco
tormentati per decidere dove
metterla. Vicino
alla porta no, né in fondo
alle scale, e neppure
giù al cancello. Lessero riviste,
credo, ricordarono visite
lontane a ville inglesi e svizzere.
Infine un giorno fu portata
da una cantina una cassetta di latta
grande come un volume di enciclopedia,
fu dipinta di verde, e quasi ormai
mimetizzata tra l'edera e il fogliame
dei piccoli pinastri e del susino
fu appesa al muro di cinta, che separa
il giardino dalla via stretta e ripida, un
sentiero che cade verso la città.

Era lì, introvabile e perciò
forse elegante, con così poca
prosopopea, senza neppure i nostri
nomi scritti su: tra due tronchi
divisi a fionda di pinastri giovani,
incastrata nella pietra grigia, all'ombra
di allori e di oleandri.

SPRING

The Gecko in the Mailbox

Do you remember how late, after almost
two months of consultations,
we got a mailbox?
It was a funny thing. The landlords,
elderly, wishing to keep high up
the decorum of their property,
the walls freshly whitewashed
the escutcheons up high, the long
battlements, the garden. . .
They were uncertain, a little tormented, in deciding
where to put it. Not near the door,
nor at the bottom of the stairs,
nor down by the gate. They read reviews,
I think, remembering
remote visits to English and Swiss
villas.
Finally one day, a tin mailbox
was brought up from the cellar,
a mailbox as large as an encyclopedia volume;
it was painted green, and almost
camouflaged between the ivy and the branches
it was hung on the wall
separating the garden from the narrow
and steep streets, a path
falling down toward the city.

It was there, impossible to find, therefore
elegant perhaps, modest, without
even our names written on it:
between two trunks
divided by a sling of young pines
set in gray stone, in the shade
of the laurels and the oleanders.

Il vento ci portò presto ricurvi
aghi bruciati, rametti, foglie
tagliate e ingiallite. Ci cadde
pioggia: e un ragno
da un giorno all'altro ci stese
nell'angolo una ragnatela, comoda
e obliqua come un'amaca.

E divenne in primavera la casa
di chi sai tu, era
inevitabile. "Si affezionano,
ritornano ogni giorno al caldo e al sole
in un punto, sempre in quello, c'è
una specie di bussola che li guida."
E si appostano, e aspettano
lì, solitari, più
fermi di una spilla su una cravatta.
Divenne la casa di un geco, la nostra
cassetta delle lettere, di uno appena
nato, e non so perché
solo, senza padre né madre né fratelli
un gechino ancora rosa,
traslucido quasi, e morbido,
corto più di un mignolo, magro
appena meno di una foglia.
Sapeva guizzare via, ma controvoglia
e a piccoli scatti incerti, incespicando.
Ricordi le sue zampine, fatte
di coriandoli, la sua coda
tenera, inerte?

Chi era, perché lì solo, la sua scelta
di abitare nella nostra cassetta
tra plichi e lettere e libri, ne
parlavamo. "Ma crescerà" dicevi "io
non potrò mai più
aprirla per la posta, avrò
troppa paura." Io temporeggiavo.

The wind soon brought in it
curved burned needles, twigs, cut
and yellow leaves. Rain fell in it.
And from one day to the other, a spider
stretched a web in the corner, as comfortable,
as oblique as a hammock.

And in spring it became the house
of you-know-who, it was inevitable.
"They get fond of the place,
they return every day to the heat and the sun,
to one spot, always the same, there is
some sort of compass guiding them."
And there they lurk, there
they wait, more still than a pin
on a tie.
It became the house of a gecko,
our mailbox, an infant gecko,
who knows why alone,
without mother or father or brother,
a little gecko still pink,
almost translucent, and soft,
shorter than a little finger,
as thin as a leaf.
He knew how to dart away, but unwillingly, with little
uncertain sprints,
stumbling.
Do you remember his little feet
made of confetti, his tender
inert tail?

Who he was, why he was there alone,
his choice to live in our mailbox
between packages and letters and books—
we talked about that. "But will he grow?"
you would say. " I will never be able
to get the mail,
I will be scared." I stalled for time.

Poi un giorno — sei sicura
che non sia stato un sogno? tu mi hai detto
d'averlo preso per la coda tra
le punte delle dita
d'averlo portato in mezzo all'edera
più folta, che fosse
smarrita la strada per ritornare.

Era così minuto, così indifeso
che hai potuto toccarlo?
Suo padre ti avrebbe terrorizzato,
fatto gridare aiuto:
con lui neonato hai avuto
un rapporto così, quasi amoroso?

Ma è scomparso davvero e non è più
tornato. Io per un po'
l'ho rimpianto.
E ho aperto con cautela la cassetta
ancora per qualche giorno. Intanto
lui chi sa dove era andato
a chi si era "affezionato"
che ricordo portava delle tue dita
con sé.

Then one day—are you sure
it was not a dream?—you said
you had taken him by the tail
with your fingertips,
and that you took him to the middle
of the thickest ivy, so that he would
lose the way of the return.

He was so tiny, so defenseless—
how could you touch him?
His father would have scared you,
would have made you cry for help:
with him, newborn as he was, did you have
an almost, so to speak, amorous rapport?

But he really disappeared and never
came back. I missed him for a while.
And for a few days I still
opened the mailbox with caution.
Meanwhile who knows
where he had gone, to whom "he had become attached,"
what memory of your fingertips
he had taken
with him.

ESTATE

Gli scoiattoli al Central Park

Lo dicono anche le guide turistiche
che ci sono gli scoiattoli al Central Park.[1]
E noi ne avevamo visto uno
solo, uno magro, grigio come
un topo di città e con una piccola
coda bisunta, che restava
ai piedi di un tronco d'albero
nell'ombra, fermo come un malato,
come un sopravvissuto.

C'era sembrato anche lui derelitto
come gli uomini che seggono sui marciapiedi
al fondo di Prince Street
con accanto il sacchetto di carta
tutto pieghe intorno al collo
della bottiglia,
come i piccioni che raspano
l'erba, la fanghiglia del Battery
Park confinante con i pontili.

Non ricordo se l'avevamo festeggiato.
Il dubbio che fosse un topo non era subito
andato via: quella coda
così poco gloriosa
ti aveva insospettito,
quel pelo così poco
folto, quel fare mesto,
quello starsene solo.

Ma quest'estate, invece! Sono in volo
gli scoiattoli, da ramo a ramo, da
cespuglio a cespuglio, sui sentieri
dove qualche foglia è già

---

[1] *Central Park*...: a Manhattan, come gli altri luoghi ricordati nella poesia (Prince Street, Battery Park, Broadway, Lincoln Center).

SUMMER

The Squirrels in Central Park

Even the tourist guides say
that there are squirrels in Central Park.[1]
We had seen one
Only, skinny, as gray as
a city mouse, with a dirty
little tail, who stayed
at the foot of the tree trunk
in the shade, as still as a sick person,
as a survivor.

To us, he had seemed like a derelict,
like the men sitting on the sidewalk
at the end of Prince Street
with a paper bag next to them,
all folded around the neck
of the bottle,
like the pigeons that scrape
the grass, the mud
of Battery Park where it borders the piers.

I do not remember whether we greeted him.
The doubt he might be a mouse
was not dispelled right away: that tail,
inglorious as it was,
had made you suspicious,
that hair, so thin,
his sad demeanor,
his staying alone.

But this summer, instead! The squirrels
are flying from branch to branch,
from bush to bush, on the paths
where some leaves have already fallen

---

[1] Central Park in Manhattan is remembered in this poem by Conte, as well as Prince Street, Battery Park, Broadway, and Lincoln Center.

caduta, sui prati, intorno
alle panchine, a quella grata
che dà sul cortiletto delle altalene
scoiattoli dappertutto, tanti, come
neppure un bosco ne ospita.
Guardali bene:
non hai perplessità ora: fai festa
anche tu.
Sono fulvi questi, hanno il pelo
alto, crespo, pulito
e la coda, questa è una coda
di scoiattolo!

Ci tagliano la strada, ne scoppiano
certi rami di quercia,
vanno in coppia
per i tronchi, e poi
forse bisticciano, non vedi?
Piovono foglie, ghiande come
grandine al suolo.

Quando sono lassù, sembra che volino
proprio, che inseguano
la vetta di ogni ramo teso contro
l'azzurro del mattino per scomparire
ma verso
dove?

E uno di passaggio a terra
uno solo, lento, che
sentì i nostri piedi si fermò
quasi estatico, le zampe
corte e forti appena un po'
divaricate, arcuato il dorso, il capo
ancora più culminante in un nasino
nero, credo: si fermò
a guardarci: e non ci
capì, non volle
comunicarci nulla,
muto come le zolle della terra

on the meadows, around
the benches, around that grating
looking in on the little courtyard with the swings,
squirrels everywhere, so many,
more than a forest could house.
Look at them well!
Do not be puzzled now: you too,
celebrate!
They are red, these, they have crisp,
tall, clean hair, and the tail,
this is a real tail
of a squirrel!

They cut across our path, some oak branches
explode with them,
they go through the trunks
in couples, then maybe
they fight, don't you see?
Leaves and acorns rain down
to the ground like hail.

When they are up there, they look like
they are flying, running after the summit
of every branch stretching toward
the blue morning sky, to disappear,
but
in what direction?

And one passing by on the ground,
one alone, a slow one, who heard
our steps, stopped,
almost ecstatic, his short,
strong legs barely
spread apart,
his back arched, his head
culminating in a black
little nose, I think. He did not
understand us,
he did not communicate anything to us,
as silent as the clods of dirt,

come i raggi del sole sulle foglie.
Quanti erano quel giorno! Le folle
sulla Settima sin giù
dove incontra Broadway, imitavano
quelle?
O i frettolosi che arrivavano al Lincoln Center
in bicicletta con la borsa di libri
o ne uscivano a fumare una sigaretta
d'in piedi?

"Credilo: sono scoiattoli, non hanno
niente a che fare con noi:
né quello solitario di anni fa
né i tanti di questa
estate:
né il vecchio malinconico, né i festanti
di oggi. È bello che ci siano
loro qua, che saltino così
improvvisi: raggi del mattino
arricciati sembrano
di un sole piccolino, un gomitolo
di luce."

as the sun rays on the leaves.
How many there were that day!
The crowds—from Seventh Avenue
down to Broadway—did they
imitate the crowds?
Or the hasty people who arrived
at Lincoln Center bicycling with a bag of
books, or who came out of it to smoke
a cigarette?

"Believe me: they are squirrels, they have
nothing to do with us:
neither the solitary one of several years ago,
nor the many
this summer;
neither the old melancholy one, nor
the ones making merry today.
It's lovely that they are
here, that they jump up
so suddenly: so curled
they look like the morning rays
of a tiny sun, like a skein
of light."

AUTUNNO

La cavalletta sulle scale

Non fu empio il mio piede: si fermò
in tempo per non cancellarti, cavalletta.
Non so da che cosa ti avvertii:
so che passò la fretta di rientrare

a casa: e mi curvai, a guardarti:
eri regale, delicata, assente
come nessuna donna è: muta
come un monile, ma insistente

tentavi lo scalino troppo alto
per te. Ti ci avvicinavi con delle zampe
che parevano passive, meccaniche, tanto
erano oscillanti e filiformi, e cominciavi

di sbieco la risalita, con una specie
di fatica, di impassibile
tremore. Più lunga e magra del mio
indice e chiara, color avorio, è

possibile? Salivi e poi tornavi
giù, padrona appena dei tuoi movimenti;
e io sempre più curvo sino a guardarti
negli occhi lucenti, nerissimi.

Eri forse così vecchia, o l'autunno
iniziava a poggiare su di te
la sua mano che fa freddi,
fragili? Ma perché volevi salire

quello scalino, perché ti affaticavi per
raggiungere la cima, dove c'è
la mia casa, e perché mi hai fermato,
per dire cosa?

AUTUMN

The Grasshopper on the Staircase

My foot was not impious: it stopped
in time not to erase you, grasshopper.
I do not know what made me realize you were there.
I know that I was no longer in a hurry

to get home, and I bent over to look at you.
You were regal, delicate, as absent
as no woman can ever be: as silent
as an ornament. But persistently

you attempted to scale the staircase
too high for you. You approached it
with legs that seemed passive, mechanical,
oscillating and thread-like,

and you started to climb again, sideways,
with a sort of fatigue, of impassive tremor.
Longer and thinner than my index finger,
and light, ivory-colored, is it possible?

You climbed and then you came
down again, barely mastering your movement,
and I bent over more and more
to look at your shining black jet eyes.

Where you perhaps too old, or was autumn
starting to place on you
its hand that makes us cold,
fragile? But why did you want

to climb that step, why did you toil
to reach that summit where my house is,
and why did you stop me—
to tell me what?

LE STAGIONI DI FLORA

THE SEASONS OF FLORA[1]

---

[1] Flora, the Roman goddess of flowering and blossoming plants.

Flora, barbara
ragazza degli Oschi e dei Sabini
correvi nei boschi di prima
delle acropoli e delle vie
sui pendii di querce e di lecci
tra le felci rapide, tra i lenti
salici che scendevano sin quasi
alle spiagge.

Flora, veloce più di una cerva, barbara
ragazza, portavi un mantello che io
so: d'inverno era bianco di neve
ma poi ci nascevano primule
franate al confine dei campi,
le docili, azzurre, screziate
corolle dei colchici.

Di primavera, il mantello
ti si alzava a volo sulle spalle
per il vento amante che ti inseguiva:
ed era una tremula valle
di anemoni, iris, narcisi,
pareti di roccia di rose.

D'estate si impolverava; toccava
terra, radeva
le stoppie ed il greto, il fango
secco degli stagni.
E ci crescevano i ginestroni,
i cimelli piumosi di un canneto.

L'autunno era tutto campanule
quei calici blu fragili
che hanno brividi, e a mille
a mille le mani di ogni sera
chiudono.

Flora, barbarian maiden
of the Oscans and the Sabines,
you used to run in the woods—
before the acropolis and the streets existed—
on slopes of oak and holm-trees,
amidst rapid ferns, amidst slow
willows that came almost down
to the shores.

Flora, swifter than a doe, barbarian
maiden, you wore a familiar mantle:
in winter it was white with snow.
But then primulas sliding to the edge of the fields
were born in it,
and the blue, docile,
speckled corollas of the colchicum too.

In spring, your mantle
soared in flight over your shoulders
as the amorous wind pursued you—
and it became a valley
trembling with anemones, iris and narcissus,
a rock-wall of roses.

In the summer, your mantle got dusty.
It touched the earth, it razed
the stubble and the river bed, the dry mud
of the ponds.
There used to grow big bushes of Scotch broom,
and the feathery tops of a cane bracket.

Autumn was all campanulas,
those fragile blue calyxes
that have a thousand shivers, that by the thousands
close
the hands of every evening.

Flora, più alta di un'arpa, barbara
ragazza degli Oschi e dei Sabini
che hai avuto nei boschi
tra i cinghiali e gli agrifogli i primi
templi, tra i cespugli
di rosmarino e di lentischio i primi
altari, ascolta.

Ti chiamo io flamine[1]
tardo e da poco.
Non ho che un fuoco,
questo,
da accenderti.

---

[1] *flamine*: dal latino *flamen*, sacerdote romano.

Flora, taller than a harp, barbarian
maiden of the Oscans and the Sabines,
you, who were the first to have temples
erected to you in the woods,
among boars and bushes
of holly, rosemary and lentisk,
listen!

I call you, slow
and lowly priest that I am.
I have but one fire,
this one,
to light for you.

INVERNO

Neve sugli aloe

È stato freddissimo: forse
da trent'anni non nevicava più
così sul Meditteraneo.
Prima vennero il gelo e la galaverna.[1]
Bruciarono, come si può
bruciare senza ustioni né fiamme,
si ingrigirono, fatti friabili
e poi cavi, inconsistenti
al tatto, rattrappiti,
più immobili dei morti,
i carciofi negli orti, le buganvillee
dei parchi, i geranei.

Anche qualche muretto di sostegno
construito in pietra viva franò.
Le pietre ruzzolarono, terriccio
si sparse come farina da una ferita
del sacco.

La neve scese a lungo: per qualche ora
l'Aurelia su Capo Berta fu chiusa.[2]
Ci fu silenzio, come c'è le volte
che si pensa un miracolo o si attende.
Poi smise, era buio oramai, il giardino
un vasto, biancheggiante, sconosciuto
giardino,
remoto anche se pochi
scalini
bastavano a raggiungerlo.

Certi alberi reggevano la neve
come se ci fossero stati abituati.
I cedri del Libano, bene

---

[1] *galaverna*: formazioni di ghiaccio sui rami degli alberi.
[2] *Capo Berta*: promontorio che divide Oneglia da Diano Marina.

WINTER

The Snow on the Aloes

It was bitter cold: for some
thirty years it had not snowed
like this on the Mediterranean.
First came the frost and the icicles.
They burnt, as one can burn
without wound or flames.
The artichokes in the orchards, the bouganvilleas
of the parks, the geraniums
made crumbly
then hollow, insubstantial
to the touch—they all became gray,
shrunk, more still than the dead.

Even some rock walls fell down.
The stones crumbled, dirt
was strewn about, like flour pouring
from the wound
of a sack.

The snow fell for a long time, for a few hours
the Aurelia Road on Cape Berta was closed.[1]
There was the silence reigning
when one thinks about or waits for a miracle.
Then it stopped, it was dark then, and the garden
became a vast, whitening, unknown
garden,
remote even if one
could reach it
with only a few steps.

Some trees supported the snow
as if they had been used to it
The cedars of Lebanon, the oak trees,

---

[1] Capo Berta is a promontory separating Oneglia from Diano Marina. Aurelia is the name of the ancient Roman road.

le querce, i crespi
cipressi incolonnati, gli allori
più alti, i biancospini, i nespoli
dalle foglie simili a chiglie
di gozzi.

Sopra gli altri la neve dondolava,
non lo so se era lei che non voleva
o se proprio non ci riusciva
a prendere posizione:
sui rami dei pini marittimi
protesi come bracci di candelabri
e aguzzi su in cima di ciuffi
interi di aghi, lì come
poteva fermarsi?
E sulle foglie delle palme
libiche, simili ai raggi
di una ruota del carro
del sole
dove poteva posarsi, quella straniera?
Dondolava così, tra ripetuti
crolli.

Sugli aloe, qui già un poco fioriti
con le loro impervie spighe rosse
volle insediarsi, premere
con il suo peso che non
si immagina sia così
rovinoso.

Li ho visti in una stazione, poteva
essere quella di Vado, di Varazze
gli aloe strozzati, marciti,
loro così sempre vividi
così sempre intenti a un miraggio
di oasi, così memori
del sangue e della carne che ha la
luce,
erano atroci, tanto
piegati da un dolore che non potevano

the crisp cypresses lined up like columns,
the tallest laurels, the hawthorns, and the medlars
that have leaves
like the keels
of fishing smacks.

The snow oscillated on the other trees.
I don't know whether it did not want to
or if it really could not
take a stand:
on the branches of the maritime pines
stretched out like the arms of candelabra
and sharp on the top of whole
tufts of needles—how could
it stop there?
And on the leaves of the Lybian
palm trees, similar to the rays
of the sun's cartwheel,
where could that stranger
land?
It swung like this, between repeated
falls.

The snow decided to settle on the aloes
already flowering a little
with their impervious red spikes,
to press down on them with a weight
no one could have imagined
so ruinous.

I saw them at the train station, it could have been
that of Vado or Varazze,[1]
the strangled, rotting aloes,
they—always so vivid,
always so intent upon the mirage
of an oasis, so mindful
of the blood and the flesh that has
light—

---

[1] *Varazze, Vado*: Towns on the Western Riviera in Liguria.

capire, aggrumati
in una ressa mortale, lividi, fradici,
come se universale ormai, ordinato
dalle costellazioni fosse il marciume.
Sugli aloe si accaniva, era
crudele la neve, una vendicatrice:
ma di che torti?

Aloe morti a Varazze, a Vado, nei miei
ricordi d'inverno, sogni
sconfitti, silenziose
vittime.

they were atrocious, bent over
by a pain they could not
understand, clotted
in a lethal throng, livid, rotten,
as if rot were universally
ordained by the constellations.
The snow was cruel
with the aloes, like an implacable avenger:
but of what wrongs?

Dead aloes at Varazze, at Vado,
in my winter memories, defeated
dreams, silent
victims.

PRIMAVERA

Ginestre intorno all'autostrada

Un giorno qui che è maggio te ne accorgi
guidando l'automobile verso Genova:
di là del parabrezza in corsa appaiono
insensibili, immense, le ginestre.
Sono lì, sregolate
come fascine di luce
piovuta e rappresa, come
covoni rovesciati, spezzati
favi.

Per loro non c'è il tempo dell'attesa.
Non si vedevano sino a qualche settimana
fa, nessuno le aspettava loro, selvatiche.
Dov'erano, dove lo condensavano
tutto questo loro bagliore
tutti gli steli, tutto il fiore
cromato, quasi spinoso
oggi glorioso più che una visione?

Vanno le automobili, si lasciano
indietro i caselli: S. Bartolomeo
del Cervo, Pietra, Finale.
Qui non grandeggia il mare quasi
più: è come in fondo a una gola
che non finisce, è un riverbero cavo,
un presentimento.
Le valeriane, anche loro
nate da un giorno all'altro,
invadenti, flessibili, spumose
bordano il guard-rail
coprono le piazzuole
cadono nei botri,
dovunque trovano una zolla
crescono.

SPRING

The Scotch Broom around the Freeway

On any day in May, driving to Genoa,
you become aware of them:
beyond the running windshield they appear
insensitive, immense, the Scotch broom bushes.
They are there, unruly
like sheaves of light
rained down and clotted,
like overturned sheaves of grain, like
broken honeycombs.

For them, there is no time for waiting.
They could not be seen until a few weeks ago,
nobody was waiting for them, the wild ones.
Where were they, where were they condensing
all their glare,
all their stalks and their chrome-colored
flowers, almost thorny,
today more glorious than a vision?

The cars drive on, leaving
the track stations behind: San Bartolomeo
del Cervo, Pietra, Finale.[1]
Here the sea hardly dominates:
it is like the bottom on an endless throat,
a hollow reverberation,
a forefeeling.
The valerians, they too,
born almost in one day,
invading, flexible, foamy,
they border the guardrail,
they cover the little squares,
fall down into deep ditches,
grow wherever they can find
a little dirt.

---

[1] Other Ligurian towns.

Ginestre e valeriane, colline
instabili, a capofitto
nella primavera
ginestre, costellazioni labili,
castelli aridi, torrenti
di luce in piena.
Siete antiche? Conoscevate
le dune costiere, le grotte,
le dee senza nome, l'altare
di pietra e notte?
Scalavate già Capo Berta
quando al buio confinava con l'Orsa
e il giorno il carro del sole
radeva la vetta con la sua corsa?

Voi siete indomabili, credo,
non potrete mai finire.
Cadranno i viadotti sul fondovalle,
le frane fenderanno le
gallerie
forse salirà ancora il mare
dove già fu, dove ancora oggi scavano
i ragazzi giocando delle conchiglie
fossili.
Ma voi, eternate da non so
quali energie
....

Una ne è nata
la primavera scorsa sul viale
di ghiaia del giardino
chiuso da una catena
dove da tempo ormai non passa più
nessuno in automobile.
È nata dalla ghiaia, proprio,
vicino alla siepe del pittosforo,
all'ombra di un cedro del Libano
dirimpetto al disegno esile che
fanno nel cielo i rami
dell'albero di canfora.

Scotch broom bushes and valerians, unstable
hills, plummeting
into the spring,
Scotch broom bushes, fleeting constellations
and arid castles, torrents of light
overflowing, streaming.
Are you ancient? Did you know
the coastal dunes, the grottoes,
the nameless goddesses, the altar
of stone and night?
Where you already climbing Capo Berta,
when it bordered on the Great Bear in the dark,
and when by day the sun's chariot
razed its summit in its course?

You are indomitable, I think,
you will never end.
The viaducts will fall on the bottom
of the valleys, the landslides will split
the galleries,
maybe the sea will climb
to its former level, where even today
the boys dig when they play
with fossilized shells.
But you, made eternal by I-do-not-know
what energies
....

One of them was born
last spring on the gravel alley
of the garden
enclosed by a gate,
where for a long time no one
has driven by.
It was really born from the gravel,
near the pittosporum hedge,
in the shade of a cedar of Lebanon
right in front of the delicate designs
that the camphor tree branches
trace in the sky.

Nata e venuta su così, spaesata,
unica, ispida, più
di spini verdi che di fiori
e ad altezza
d'uomo, oramai.

La saluto passando la solitaria.
"Le tue compagne su sull'autostrada
sarebbero capaci di spezzare
l'asfalto
di svellere il loro sole grande, caldo,
portarlo a confinare con il mare
e l'aria?"

Born and arrived like this, displaced,
unique, bristling,
more with green thorns than flowers—
and now already
as tall as man.

I greet her passing by, the solitary one.
"Would your companions on the freeway
be able to break
the asphalt,
to uproot that great, warm sun of theirs,
to bring it to the edge
of the sea and the air?"

ESTATE

I girasoli sul Rio Grande

Avrei voluto saperne il nome indiano:
erano come girasoli, i loro
stessi occhi globosi, colmi
di nostalgia per il cielo
gli stessi petali gialli, raggianti,
incoronanti, e mesti: lo stesso stelo
flessibile, come in attesa
dei soffi dei venti.
Ma cresciuti stranamente poco
da terra, con una corolla
mai più larga di una mano chiusa
a pugno: e se ne stavano insieme
in magri cespugli, affacciati
in tanti sui bordi della highway,
sul ciglio roccioso del fiume.

È rosso di pietra tagliata
da un lungo coltello di alba
è verde di pini franati
sul limpido greto, il Rio Grande.

E noi lo costeggiavamo: al culmine
di una salita e di una svolta
che dava nel vuoto
del cielo
così a precipizio, infinito
ci apparve il deserto, delirio
di un mare senza mare.

Come chi sente di riacquistare
la vista dopo una lunga cecità
di colpo, urlammo, credo:
sorretti da rocce che di lontano
sembravano tronchi sfaldati

SUMMER

The Sunflowers of the Rio Grande[1]

I would have liked to know their Indian name:
they were like sunflowers, the same
globose eyes, filled with
longing for the sky,
the same yellow petals, radiant,
crown-like and sad: the same flexible
stem, as if waiting
for gusts of wind.
Yet strangely grown but little
from the ground, with a corolla
never larger than a closed
fist: they huddled together
in thin bushes, leaning in many clusters
on the edges of the highway,
on the rocky brink of the river.

The Rio Grande is red with stone
cut by the long knife of dawn,
green with pines sliding
down to the clear river-bed.

And we were coasting along it: to the top
of a climb and of a turn
that looked out on the empty
sky,
thus suddenly, headlong, infinite,
the desert appeared to us, a delirium
of a sea without a sea.

Like those who feel they are regaining
sight after a long blindness,
suddenly, I believe, we shouted:
supported by rocks that from afar
looked like the flaking trunks

---

[1] This poem was written during Conte's first trip to New Mexico.

di cono, eccoli, gli altopiani
solenni, piallati, impraticabili
come neppure gli altari sono.
Nessun albero più: ma il verde
riarso di erbe ispide, di fiori
gremiti come le ginestre,
cespugli sfiniti dall'aridità,
più scavati del lentischio, rare
yucche dalle foglie ferrigne, dentellate
e loro, i piccoli girasoli.

Lungo un altopiano, quella linea
franta e allungata d'ombra
che sembrava lì disegnata da un eclisse
parziale, impazzito
segnava le sponde
sprofondate del Rio Grande
giù dal Colorado.

Tutto era di un rosso scurito
da verdi spinosi, opachi, quasi
di polvere, e dall'azzurro
di un cielo basso, a portata
di mano, dov'erano annidate
per voli veloci le nuvole.

Piccoli girasoli d'estate.
Piccoli e cresciuti
a cespugli. Ricordate
ancora i passi dei guerrieri
e dei cacciatori sul sentiero
dei cervi e del vento,
le preghiere
alla terra, il canto
della pioggia,
la supplice attesa
del ragazzo in vetta alla collina
tutta la notte
a interrogare le nubi nere, il tuono,
le correnti dell'aria, il crepitio

of a cone, there they were, the plateaus,
solemn, planed—more unapproachable
than even altars.
No more trees: nothing but the burnt
green of bristly grass, of flowers
crowded like Scotch broom,
bushes exhausted by aridity,
more hollowed than lentisk, rare yuccas
with ferruginous indented leaves,
and then they, the little sunflowers.

Along a plateau, that broken
long line of shadow
that seemed sketched there
by a crazed,
partial eclipse,
marked the sunken shores of the Rio Grande
down from Colorado.

All was of red, a red made dark
by thorny, opaque, almost
ashen green hues, and by the blueness
of a low sky, close at hand,
where the clouds nested
ready for swift flights.

Small summer sunflowers.
Small and growing
in thickets. Do you still remember
the steps of the warriors,
the hunters following the path
of the deer and the wind,
do you remember
the prayers
to the earth, the song
of the rain,
the suppliant waiting
of the boy on the summit of the hill
all night long,
questioning the black clouds, the thunder,

delle foglie spinose della yucca,
i vostri ciechi occhi
globosi, colmi di nostalgia
per il cielo?

the air currents, the crackling
of the thorny leaves of the yucca—
your blind globose eyes
filled with longing for the sky?

AUTUNNO

La vite del Canada

Nel giardino di sempreverdi, tu sola porti
le accese, crollanti insegne dell'autunno
al cielo: sei rossa come il sole dei tramonti
ed è veloce il tuo sfacelo.

Risali i cipressi, ti aggrappi alle spalliere
d'edera, abbracci il giovane ulivo:
loro non cambiano, non cadono, sei
tu condannata: resterà vivo

il giardino senza di te: i tuoi acini
scuri, secchi, impolverati
non giungeranno mai alla gioia del vino.
Così accadrà anche di noi.

Rimarrà tutto come prima
quando noi sanguinando ce ne andremo
e anche sognare, allora lo sapremo
che non vale, che è vano, vite del

Canada.

AUTUMN

The Virginia Creeper

In the garden of the evergreens, you alone carry
the burning, crumbling insignia of autumn
to the sky: you are as red as the sun of the sunsets
and you fall apart quickly.

You climb cypresses, you attach yourself
to ivy espaliers, you embrace the young olives:
they do not change, they do not fall, *you* are
condemned: the garden will remain alive

without you. Your grapes, dark, dry and dusty,
will never reach the joy of wine.
The same will be of us.

Everything will remain as it was before,
when, bleeding, we will depart,
and even dreaming, we will know then,
even sleeping is of no use, it is vain, Virginia

Creeper.

LE STAGIONI DI ERMES

THE SEASONS OF HERMES

Mi chiedo: "che cosa è la mia
anima? Quali vie ha? Quali
parole? È come tra i pini del Capo
il sole, la sua scia sul mare
intoccabile, accecante, molteplice,
in un movimento che non ha
scopo?

È come l'acqua che
scende verso le origini
o como il fuoco, che cerca
la vertigine dell'altezza?"

E tu sei con me, con un gesto
alato mi chiami, in questo
tardo pomeriggio che potrebbe
essere di qualunque stagione:
un giovane bellissimo, dall'abito
di Messaggero, un sorriso indecifrabile,
straniero, come di chi ha viaggiato
oltrecielo.

Tu le sai delle anime le vie.
E io ti conosco: sei Ermes.

I ask myself: "What is my soul?[1]
What ways does it have?
What words? Is it like the sun
among the pinetrees of the Cape, its wake
on the sea, blinding, untouchable,
multiple, in a movement
that has no aim?

Is it like the water falling
toward its origin, or like the fire
that looks for the vertigo
of height?"

And you are with me, you call me
with a winged gesture, in this late
afternoon that could be in any
season: a handsome youth dressed like a Messenger,
an indecipherable, foreign
smile, like that of one
who has traveled
beyond the sky.

You know the ways of the souls.
And I know you: you are Hermes.

---

[1] Hermes: messenger god, who also led the souls to Hades.

INVERNO

L'Insegnante

"Che cosa dirai stamattina?"
Che cosa? Che è inverno, ho incontrato
due cani su un viadotto, contromano
correvano, all'altezza
del guard-rail, con le bocche
aperte ma nere, silenziose
come i primi di una invisibile muta
in cerca di che cosa, lassù?
Ai bordi l'asfalto era bianco,
ci si era posata la neve.

Parla tu per me,[1] una
volta. Entra nell'aula
con i sandali alati, con i tuoi
sorrisi acuti come smorfie, incantali
tu i ragazzi, forse ti aspettano.
Racconta le tue avventure,[2]
le furberie per cui
di te si disse: "è un dio!"
l'incontro con la tartaruga, il tuo
modo di convincerla a donarti
il guscio, quello li farà ridere; e il furto
della mandria, lo
stratagemma per sconvolgere le
impronte.

Tocca loro la fronte
con il caduceo.
Ci sono ragazze pronte
alla menzogna e alla magia.
Mostra loro i reami

---

[1] *Parla tu...*: Ermes.
[2] *Racconta...*: nel IV *Inno omerico* si racconta che Ermes, appena nato, uccise una tartaruga e, tendendo sul guscio sette corde, inventò la cetra. Subito dopo rubò cinquanta buoi dalla mandria di Apollo e, per confondere le tracce, invertì gli zoccoli degli animali.

WINTER

The Teacher

"What will you say this morning?"
What? That it's winter, that I met
two dogs on the viaduct, that they were running
on the wrong side of the road
at the level of the guard-rail,
with open, black mouths, silent,
like the first vanguard of an invisible pack,
in search of what, up there?
At the sides, the asphalt was white,
the snow had covered it.

Speak for me, once.[1]
Enter the classroom
with your winged sandals,
your smile as sharp as a grimace,
bewitch the boys, maybe they are waiting for you.
Tell them your adventures,[2]
the ruses for which
they said of you: "He is a god,"
the encounter with the tortoise, the way
you persuaded it to give you
its shell—that will make them laugh!—and the theft
of the herd, the trick
of turning
their hoof prints around.

Touch their foreheads
with your caduceus.
There are girls ready
for lies and for magic.
Show them the vast

---

[1] Line 11 refers to Hermes.
[2] The fourth Homeric Hymn recounts that Hermes, as soon as he was born, killed a turtle and invented the lyre by tying seven strings to its shell. Soon after that, he stole fifty oxen from Apollo's herd, and, to confuse the tracks, he turned the animals' hooves backwards.

ampli del vento come non fanno
libri né carte geografiche:
portali all'Egeo, all'Oceano
indiano: indica loro le città,
tienile sulla palma della tua
mano: Sidone, Pergamo, Ecbatana.
Sii musica per loro, inventa
strumenti ancora nuovi.
Insegna loro ad amare ciò che si muove
rapido sotto il sole.

Io non so dire che dell'inverno, di come
attendevo l'inverno io:
dei limpidi mattini costruiti
di pietre di muraglioni di vie in salita
e cupole nella mia città,
degli orti tra le case, dei fichi stecchiti.
Dire la mia verità:
il carrugio degli ebrei dove son nato
l'affresco della Vergine su in cima
i poveri che scendevano dalla via
stretta, detta "a Strà".
Per ogni luce fioca a una finestra
ogni sera pensavo a un dolore,
non sapevo di chi, e perché sentivo
pietà.

La sciarpa da ufficiale di picchetto
di mio padre, il suo passo diritto
su per le scale di lavagne, nere.
 "Eri un ragazzo, non dimenticarlo
il tuo sogno di allora
e quanto di esso si è compiuto poi:
potrai insegnare il sogno? Sei
arrivato, guarda, la neve
è anche qui,
spalata ai margini del parcheggio
di Piazza Eroi."

kingdoms of the wind as no book,
no map can.
Take them to the Aegean sea, to the
Indian ocean. Holding them
in the palm of your hand,
point out the cities: Sidon, Pergamum, Ecbatana.
Be music for them, invent
instruments all new.
Teach them to love all that moves
swiftly under the sun.

I can only speak of winter, of how
I used to wait for winter:
of limpid mornings, made of the rocks
of retaining walls in winding streets,
domes of my town,
of the orchards between the houses, of the dried up fig-trees.
To tell my truth:
the *carrugio* of the Jews where I was born,[1]
the fresco of the Virgin up on top,
the poor people coming down the narrow
lane, called "a Strà."
For every glimmering light at a window,
every night, I thought of a sorrow—
I did not know whose—and why I felt
compassion.

My father's orderly-officer's sash,
his straight step
up the black slate steps.
"You were a boy, do not forget
your childhood dream,
and how much of it was fulfilled later:
will you be able to teach them the dream? You have
arrived, look, the snow
is here also,
shoveled all the way to the edge
of Piazza Eroi."

---

[1] *Carrugio*: In Ligurian dialect, it is a long narrow lane, often flanked by tall buildings.

PRIMAVERA

Il Poeta

Non sapevo che cosa è un poeta
quando guidavo alla guerra i carri
e il cavallo Xanto mi parlava.
Ma è passata come una cometa

l'età ragazza di Ettore e di Achille:
non sono diventato altro che un uomo:
la mia anima si cerca ora nelle acque
e nel fuoco, nelle mille

famiglie dei fiori e degli alberi
negli eroi che io non sono
nei giardini dove tutta la pena

di nascere e morire è così leggera.
Forse il poeta è un uomo che ha in sé
la crudele pietà di ogni primavera.

SPRING

The Poet

I did not know what a poet was
when I used to drive chariots to war
and the horse Xantos talked to me.
But like a comet the youthful age

of Hector and Achilles has gone by.
I became nothing but a man:
now my soul looks for itself in the water
and in the fire, and in the thousand

families of flowers and trees,
in the heroes that I am not,
in the gardens where all the pain

of being born and dying is so light.
Maybe the poet is a man who holds inside himself
the cruel pity of each spring.

ESTATE

Il Viaggiatore

Il viaggiatore conosce bene i labili
rapporti che ogni terra ha con le nubi.
Non sa che cosa li determini:
se sia il vento, la direzione
che hanno fiumi e montagne
la presenza di altopiani, di colline
il sole più sfolgorante o più
appannato, la distanza dai
mari.
Tra Albuquerque e Santa Fe certe mattine[1]
il cielo cala quasi in modo che
le nubi corrano tra cespugli e spine.
Hanno la casa su vulcani
spenti, tra rocce
che fanno gobbe, ali, artigli
tra dune di terriccio che
fiori stenti e ruvidi
intaccano, su pianori
verdi e vasti, sorretti
da tronchi coni di pietra lassù.
Le nuvole ci volano o ci stanno
inginocchiate.
Vegliano sui tre Pueblo di
S. Domingo, Cochiti, S. Felipe,
deserto indiano d'estate.

Più a nord, verso il Colorado
sono ancora più rapide, più oblique, e più
in movimento.

Sul massiccio del Sangre de Cristo
lasciano impronte
di un nero che rasenta

---

[1] *Albuquerque e Santa Fe*: città del Nuovo Messico, negli Stati Uniti.

SUMMER

The Traveler[1]

The traveler knows well the fleeting
relation that each land has with the clouds.
He does not know what determines it:
the wind, the direction
of the rivers and mountains
the presence of plateaus, plains, hills
the sun now more blazing, now more blurred,
the distance from the
seas.
Between Albuquerque and Santa Fe some mornings
the sky drops so low
that the clouds almost hang
between bushes and thorns.
They dwell on extinct
volcanoes, among rocks
that form humps, wings and claws,
between dunes of mold corroded
by starved rough flowers on the green
and vast plateaus, held up there
by truncated cones of stone.
There the clouds fly or hover,
kneeling.
They watch over the three pueblos of
Santo Domingo, Cochiti and San Felipe,
over the Indian desert in the summer.

More to the North, towards Colorado,
they are even more rapid, more oblique
and more in movement.

On the Sangre de Cristo range
they leave
black spots resembling

---

[1] Again, this poem refers to Conte's trip to the Southwest. During this trip, Conte visited San Cristobal, where the ranch and grave of D.H. Lawrence still are.

quello delle criniere.
E sulla strada che da Taos porta
a San Cristobal
fanno scorrere, svanire,
sovrapporre, saltare
macchie così scure e in un momento
mutate e tante che sembrano
una mandria di ombre
impazzite a pascolare
lì intorno.

Ogni terra ha rapporti con le nubi.
E il Viaggiatore conosce bene i labili
rapporti che ha ogni anima con il vento.

the color of horses' manes.
And on the road from Taos
to San Cristobal,
they make spots fly, vanish,
juxtapose and jump,
spots so dark and so swiftly changing—
so numerous—
as to seem like a herd
of crazed shadows,
grazing
around there.

Every land has a relationship with the clouds—
and the traveler knows well the fleeting
relationship that every soul has with the wind.

AUTUNNO

L'Amante[1]

Devoto deve essere l'amante[2]
all'autunno. Non ai venti
torbidi, che fiaccano e fanno bianchi
di meli e di susini i cieli
né alla bonaccia nuda, distesa,
dalle grandi braccia di quiete.
È devoto all'autunno perché rimane
nei raggi obliqui e lunghi di ottobre
negli orti che si spogliano
lenti tra i muri delle case
in ombra, nell'odore
nuovo di pioggia tra i pini e gli allori
qualcosa della fervida spinta cieca,
qualcosa della placata vampa
ma come assottigliato, come fatto
finalmente nitido, in una stanca
matura ricchezza, acini dorati
dimenticati sulla vite, abbaglianti
soltanto l'attimo che incontrano
il sole.

Da ragazzo, ogni sera, mi strangolava
l'ossessa primavera di carezze
cercate.
Poi, inondante, venne l'estate
con lei. Lei incolpevole, mite e
così tenue, così ardente, come
la corolla purpurea del papavero
di california, come un canneto arso d'agosto.

---

[1] "In questa poesia i dati dell'esperienza si trasferiscono in emblemi mediante l'apparizione di diverse figure femminili che alludono alla ricerca di un assoluto amoroso, anche se in chiave occidua e autunnale" (G. C.).
[2] *Devoto deve essere l'amante*: Cfr. l'*incipit* di Goethe, *Elegie romane*, IV: "Devoti siamo noi amanti, adoriamo in silenzio tutti i dèmoni [...]."

AUTUMN

The Lover[1]

The lover must be a devotee[2]
of Autumn. Not devoted to the turbid
winds that weaken and make the skies
white with apple and plum trees,
nor to the naked, stretched-out dead calm at sea
with its big arms of quietness.
He is a devoted to Autumn because it lingers
in the slanted and long October rays
in the orchards that slowly lose
their leaves between the walls of houses
in the shade, in the new scent
of rain among the pines and the laurels,
something in the fervid blind push,
something of the placated flame
but as if thinned, as if finally
cleared, in a tired
mature richness, golden grapes
forgotten in the vine, dazzling
only the minute they meet
the sun.

As a child, every evening, the obsessed
spring of desired caresses
strangled me.
Then, overwhelming, summer also came.
Guiltless, mild and so
tenuous, so ardent, like the
purple corolla of the California poppy,
like a cane-thicket burnt out in August.

---

[1] "In this poem, the data of experience are transferred to emblems through the appearance of several feminine figures, alluding to the search for absolute love, even if in a Western autumnal key" (Author's note).
[2] Goethe's beginning of *Roman Elegies*, IV: "We lovers are devoted, we adore in silence all the demons [...]."

Ora, da molto, molto non conosco
più quelle due stagioni.
Io sono l'inestinguibile.
In me l'amore è passato
per rapide rovinose e per lente
acque alte: ora va sicuro, veloce
come su una piroga verso isole
di tramonto. Ora è devoto
agli dei, devoto a Zeus
che fu per Leda un fulmine
bianco-piumato, un capo
teso sopra un collo troppo
lungo, insensato in quella
vertigine polverulenta. Devoto
ad Atena, ad Artemide che non
è facile scorgere sulle rive
di un fiume o tra le superstiti
cerve di un bosco, e che nessuno
può possedere. Amore in me
è solenne, spietato come un danza
guerriera, o è appena
futile, delicato,
come geranei in una fioriera.
Io e te non esistiamo: non
chiedermelo: e forse
staremo ancora insieme, correremo
come daini alla fonte
risaliremo il torrente
come trote
sapremo nell'energia che ci muove,
nel respiro delle stelle nuove
la nostra essenza.

Amore è questo
riconoscersi in tutto, nella prima
rosa del mondo, nell'ultimo
ranuncolo, nella bassa marea, nel profondo
oceano.

For a long time now, I have not known
those two seasons.
I am the unquenchable.
In me love has gone through
ruinous rapids and slow
high waters: now it sails secure, swift
as if on a pirogue towards the sunset
islands. Now it is devoted
to the gods, devoted to Zeus
who was, for Leda, a white-feathered
lightening, a tense head
on a long neck,
senseless in that
powdery vertigo. Devoted
to Athena, to Artemis who is not easily
discernible on the banks of
a river or among the surviving
does in the wood—and whom no one
can possess. Love in me
is solemn, pitiless, like a war
dance, or barely
futile, as delicate
as a geranium in a flower bed.
You or I do not exist: do not
ask me: and maybe we will still
be together, we will run
like deer to the fountain,
we will swim upstream
like trout,
we will know our essence
in the energy that moves us
in the breath of the new stars.

Love is
recognizing oneself in everything, in the first
rose of the world, in the last
ranunculus, in the low tide, in the deep
ocean.

Io so adorare. E lei me lo chiedeva:
"io ne sono sicura, che tu adori
qualcuno, non è così?" No, non
qualcuno.
Le pietre in cerchio, i cromlech, le mura[1]
di una Micene brumosa, sospesa[2]
su ferri di cavallo neri di roccia
a picco sull'Atlantico:
i fiori asciugati a volo ai nostri piedi
da vento e sole appena usciti, il
lago solcato dalle costellazioni
di nuvole, i raggi setacciati
nel cielo dall'azzurro. Adoro
questo, io volevo
rispondere, ma dopo le porgevo
il mio pullover perché si era fatto
freddo: "Come il tempo va
veloce quando siamo insieme".
E la prendevo per mano,
giocavo ad adorarla un poco,
piano.

Devoto deve essere l'amante
a te Ermes, perché
c'è in lui una scaltrezza
candida, una smania
di ruberia e di inganno.

Perché è veloce, instabile – non
sanno i suoi vicini dove sta
andando
come non si sa degli aghi di pino
presi dalle ventate: ha il mantello
ed i sandali alati, come i tuoi.
I suoi passi dirigeranno

---

[1] *cromlech*: costruzioni megalitiche di nove pietre in cerchio.
[2] *Micene brumosa*: allusione al castello di Dun Aengus, sulla maggiore delle isole di Aran.

I know how to adore. She used to ask me:
"I'm sure you adore
someone, don't you?" No, not
someone.
The stones set in a circle, the cromlechs,[1]
the walls of a misty Mycenae, suspended[2]
on a black horseshoe-shaped rock
headlong on the Atlantic:
the flowers dried by the passing of our feet,
by the wind and the sun just come out,
the lake furrowed by constellations
of clouds, the rays that the blue light
sifts in the sky. I adore
this, I wanted to
answer, but then I handed her
my sweater because it had become
cold: "How swiftly does time fly
when we are together!"
And I took her by the hand,
I played to adore her a little,
gently.

The lover must be devoted
to you, Hermes, because
there is in him a candid
slyness, a craving
for theft and deceit.

Because he is swift, unstable—his
neighbors do not know where he
is going—
as one does not know where the pine needles go
when they are caught by gusts of wind:
he has a mantle
and winged sandals, like yours.
His steps will lead

---

[1] The "cromlechs" are meglythic constructions of nine stones set in a circle.
[2] Allusion to the castle of Don Aengus, on the largest of the Aran islands.

verso il cancello dell'Ade:[1] lì
anche le più segrete
anche le più franate
strade portano.

  Oh tu Sorella non chiedere
all'Amante Fratello altro che questa
onda che gli bagna forte e sovente
le ginocchia, e che non gli appartiene
se non come il sangue
alle vene e la notte alla luna.
Io sono l'inestinguibile.
Sono il frutto di tutto l'amore
scoppiato nelle primavere fertili
cresciuto nelle estati immobili
del mondo. Acini dorati
dimenticati sulla vite, abbaglianti
soltanto l'attimo che incontrano
il sole.

L'Amante è devoto all'autunno.

---

[1] *il cancello dell'Ade*: tra le altre sue funzioni, Ermes ha il compito di condurre le anime
verso l'Ade.

towards the gates of Hades:[1] there
lead even the most secret
the most dilapidated
roads.

O Sister, do not ask
the Lover Brother for anything
but this wave that frequent and strong
wets his knees, and that does not belong to him,
if not as blood
belongs to veins,
and the night to the moon.
I am the unquenchable.
I am the fruit of all the love
burst in the fertile springs,
grown in the still summers
of the world. Golden grapes
forgotten on the vine, dazzling
only the minute they meet
the sun.

The Lover is devoted to Autumn.

---

[1] Among his other functions, Hermes has the task of leading the souls to Hades.

PARTE SECONDA

Io le dissi: "a chi appartieni
tu che tanto risplendi?"
E lei rispose: "a me stessa
appartengo, io sono l'Unica.
Sono l'Amore, l'Amante, l'Amato.
Sono lo specchio, lo splendore e l'occhio
che guarda"

(*Imitazione da Abù Sa'ìd*)[1]

---

[1] *Abù Sa'ìd*, (Mayhana, Khurasan, 968-1048), poeta e mistico persiano, considerato "santo", usava predicare in versi; indrodusse la quartina a scopo didattico nella letteratura persiana.

PART II

I told her: "To whom do you belong,
you who shine so much?"
And she answered: "I belong
to myself, I am the Unique One.
I am Love, the Lover, the Beloved.
I am the mirror, the splendor and the beholding
eye."

(*In the manner of Abù Sa'ìd*)[1]

---

[1] *Abù Sa'ìd* (Mayhana, Khurasan, 968-1048 A.D.), Persian poet and mystic, was regarded as a "saint." He preached in verse and introduced the quatrain for didactic purposes in Persian literature.

LE STAGIONI DELL'ACQUA

THE SEASONS OF THE WATER

L'acqua assomiglia all'anima
dell'uomo. È irrequieta, non ha
posa. Si spande per vie che scendono
verso l'origine di ogni cosa.
E poi si muta l'acqua, è
dolce sino agli estuari
è salata nei mari
vola nelle nubi in cielo
dorme nelle stalattiti
specchia il sole nel velo
che fa sulle corolle
di crochi e margherite
ogni mattino.

L'acqua è eterna, non ha
destino.

Questa che vedi nel bicchiere
l'acqua-luce delle fontane
l'acqua nera delle tempeste
il fango delle frane
il torbido degli stagni
il dondolio delle onde
il tendere verso la luna
delle maree, la quieta
risacca lungo le spiagge sabbiose.

Come una cometa
di ghiacci sulla sua orbita
va l'anima, ritorna
al regno delle acque.

Water resembles
the soul of man. It is restless,
it never pauses. It spreads through ways
that go down towards the origin of everything.
And water also transforms itself.
It is sweet as far as the estuaries
It is salty in the seas.
It flies in the clouds of the sky.
It sleeps in the stalactites.
It reflects the sun in the veil
that it forms every morning
on the corollas of the crocus
and the daisies.

Water is eternal, it has no
destiny.

This you see in the glass
the water-light of the fountains
the black water of the tempests
the mud of the landslides
the turbidness of the ponds
the swinging of the waves
the stretching towards the moon
of the tides, the calm
surf along the sandy beaches.

Like a comet
of ice, the soul revolves
on its orbit, returns
to the kingdom of the water.

Oh innocente! Oh sempre
in movimento e mutevole
Madre delle correnti
marine e dei cavalloni
delle grotte e dei pesci
dei gusci e delle alghe
grembo su cui la luna
nelle veglie notturne
scende e si culla.

Oh innocente, profonda
e quieta, Giocatrice
dolce tra le palme delle sponde
tra le sabbie delle colline
tra le isole di roccia e
rovine e le isole –
giardino
specchio di alte vele, e dei
voli degli ibis.

Acqua della fine
Acqua del principio
l'anima ti attraversa
forse su nave o naufraga
tra venti immani, o forse
a nuoto, a nuoto
e lenta, come un loto,
una zattera.

O innocent one! Always
in movement and mutable!
Mother of the sea
currents and of the waves
of the grottoes and of the fish
of the shells and the seaweed—
womb on which the moon
in her nocturnal wakes
descends and swings.

O innocent one! Profound
and quiet, sweet Gambler
among the palms of the shores
among the sands of the hills
among the islands of rock and
ruin—and the garden
islands,
mirror of high sails and flights
of ibis.

Water of the end
Water of the beginning—
the soul crosses you
perhaps on a ship, or it shipwrecks
among powerful winds, or maybe
swimming, swimming
slowly, like a lotus,
like a raft.

LE STAGIONI DELLA TERRA

THE SEASONS OF THE EARTH

Non tocca terra, l'anima.
La vede come vedevamo
noi quel giardino, dall'alto
del terrazzino della nostra casa
senza individuarne
confini
senza conoscerne
i proprietari, e neppure
sapere dove aveva
l'ingresso principale.
Te lo ricordi? Di là, dall'alto
appariva così mobile
ora nuvoloso, compatto
ora sgranato, limpido
il verde del fogliame che copriva
muretti, pareti, sentieri.

C'era un'euforbia, forse
tante araucarie come
sagome di velieri
antichi, arenati
più che centenari eucalipti
cedri del Libano, e pini,
e intere famiglie di palme.

I colori che ritornavano, stagione
dopo stagione, te li ricordi?
Quello candido e torbido
della ginestra,
l'oro mutevole, ora più
a ponente ora più a levante
a volte introvabile, a volte
così bruciante delle mimose
il bianco nevoso dei ciliegi
a giugno lo scarlatto
marino nella serra delle rose.

It does not touch the earth, the soul.
I see it as we used to see
that garden, from the top
of the little terrace of our house
without defining
its borders
without knowing
its owners, not even
knowing where its main
entrance was.
Do you remember? From way up there
the green of the foliage that covered
stone, walls and paths
appeared so mobile,
now cloudy, compact
now broken down, limpid.

There was a euphorbia, maybe
many araucarias, similar to
the silhouettes of ancient
vessels, stranded—
more than centenary eucalyptus,
cedars of Lebanon and pines,
and entire families of palm trees.

The colors that returned, season
after season, do you remember them?
The white, turbid color of the
Scotch broom,
the mutable gold, so burning,
of the acacias,
now more to the
east, now more to the west
sometimes impossible to find,
the snow-white color of the cherry trees
in June, the marine
scarlet of the roses in the greenhouse.

L'azzurro dei palissandri disegnava
tra il verde come un fiume, che sorgeva
lassù e poi dilagava sino quasi
alla bordura di cipressi e tuie.

Non potevamo scenderci, ma al mattino
lo guardavamo. Era la nostra gioia.

Ci sarà ancora quel giardino? Dove
finiva? E di chi sarà
stato?
La terra, l'amore, lo sono
un Giardino che l'anima ha soltanto
sognato, a lungo?

The blue of the rosewoods delineated
the shape of a river among the greenery
that rose up there, then spread out almost
to the border of the cypresses and the *arbor vitae.*

We could not go down there, but in the morning
we used to look at it. It was our joy.

Is that garden still there? Where
did it end? To whom
did it belong?
The earth, love, are they
a Garden that the soul has only
dreamed, for a long time?

Ci pensi, non ho mai piantato un albero,
non hai mai avuto un figlio.
Tanto assomiglio al mare,
solitario, sterile.
Né un crespo cipresso, né un salice
umido e lento, né un'euforbia
diramata a delta, né un pesco
né un susino né un melo
ho mai fatto crescere, né un ramo
rosa o candido a marzo, né un piccolo
di uomo.

Come l'onda percuote la riva
senza fecondarla, senza lasciarvi
altro che alghe e consunte radici
così – non lo dici? – io percuoto
la vita.
Eppure l'ho amata, la
terra, ti ho amata.

Think of it, I never planted a tree,
I never had a child.
So much do I resemble the sea,
solitary, sterile.
I have never grown a crisp cypress,
nor a willow—humid and slow—
nor a delta-shaped euphorbia,
nor a peach, nor a plum, nor an apple-tree,
nor a branch pink or bright white in March,
nor have I ever
raised a child.

As the wave beats the shore
without impregnating it, without leaving there
anything but algae and worn roots,
thus—wouldn't you say?—I strike
life.
And yet I have loved it, the earth,
I have loved you.

LE STAGIONI DELL'ARIA

THE SEASONS OF THE AIR

Dopo, passate l'acqua e la terra, credi
che ci riconosceremo? Che gli occhi
ci aiuteranno? O ancora come due fiumi
andremo verso due diverse foci
come due tronchi d'albero staremo
immobili, ciechi alle precoci
ventate, lasciando che le foglie
tremino, crollino?

Chissà se in alto, al culmine
dell'aria
riavremo l'uno per l'altro i nostri volti,
i capelli, le mani, le carezze,
o se dovremo stare soli, come
un capitello su un prato di asfodeli.

Oh, se potessimo riconoscerci, allora,
come la nube riconosce il cielo
volando.

Later, after crossing the water and the earth,
do you think that we will recognize each other?
That our eyes will help us? Or that, like two rivers,
we will flow toward two different rivermouths?
We will be as motionless
as two tree trunks,
blind to the precocious gusts of wind,
leaving the leaves to tremble, to crumble?

Who knows if up above, at the summit
of the air,
we will regain our faces for each other,
our hair, our hands, our caresses,
or if we will have to be alone,
like a capital on a meadow of asphodels?

Oh, if we could recognize each other then,
like the clouds recognize the sky,
flying!

Ma dopo, al culmine dell'aria, l'anima
vedrà gli Angeli.
Come gemelli in corsa
su una pista dorata
come vascelli di nuvole
spinti dalla tramontana
come grappoli di glicine
spioventi da una
grata
insensibili al freddo e alla calura
alle mareggiate, ai tornado
rapidi come una mano
che si chiude
come una spada che cade
refrattari a ogni peso, inseparabili
dal loro silenzio, come
i raggi a ventaglio dai fari, come
dai loro profumi i fiori
li potremo vedere.

Non so neppure come li avranno, gli
occhi.
Se chiusi dalle ciglia come è chiuso
lo stame dentro una giovane
rosabianca
o se le avranno sfolgoranti, le
iridi.
Saranno infiniti, come
sulle sabbie di certe rive
le conchiglie
come gli aghi di pino che raccoglie
il vento e ammassa a terra, o fa
schizzare contro i vetri delle
finestre.

But later, at the climax of the air, the soul
will see the Angels.
Like twins running
on a golden track,
like vessels of clouds
pushed by the north wind
like grapes of wistaria
cascading from
a grating,
insensitive to cold and heat,
to the sea storms, to the tornadoes
as rapid as a hand
that closes,
as a sword that falls
resistant to all weight,
inseparable from their silence,
fanning out like rays of lighthouses,
we will be able to see them,
as we perceive flowers from their scent.

I do not even know what their eyes
will be like.
Whether they will be closed by eyelashes
like stamen within a young
white rose,
or will they have blazing
irises?
They will be infinite,
like seashells
on the sands of some shores,
like the pine needles the wind gathers
and heaps on the ground, to make them
splatter against the window-
panes.

Non parleranno. Nessuna
lingua sarà più necessaria.
Sono ali le loro, grandi? E
così silenziosa è anche l'aria, mentre
volano?

They will not speak. Languages
will be no longer necessary.
Are they wings, theirs, great wings? And
is the air also so silent, while
they fly?

LE STAGIONI DEL FUOCO

THE SEASONS OF THE FIRE

La fiamma assomiglia all'anima
dell'uomo: assomiglia alla rosa
più alta del roseto
al papavero che sovrasta
l'erba rasa di un campo
al minareto nel mattino
azzurro tra le foglie di palma.

La fiamma ritorna alla sua
dimora, all'alto del cielo, ai
soli.
Quella dell'incendio, della vampa
che consuma e corrode
palazzi, torri, fortezze
di guerrieri e di dei
e quella della candela
tremula che di notte
resta sul davanzale
e attende il volo
delle falene.

In alto, più leggera
dell'acqua e del gelo
con lo stesso potere
che sbianca, che fa vanire
il fiore sullo stelo
in alto, lieve
come il peduncolo delle
ciliege
come la nube
spinta dal levante
come un ramo azzurro
del palissandro a luglio.

Fiamma frontale, fuga
di fumo: agrumeti
d'inverno sotto i vulcani.

The flame resembles the soul
of man: it resembles the tallest
rose of the rosebush,
the poppy hovering above
the grass mowed in a field,
the minaret in the blue
morning among the palm leaves.

The flame returns to its dwelling,
high up in the sky,
to the suns.
The dwelling of the fires, of the flames,
consuming and corroding
palaces, towers, fortresses
of soldiers and of gods,
the dwelling of the trembling
candle that at night
remains on the windowsill
waiting for the flight
of the moths.

Higher up, lighter
than water and frost,
with the same power
that whitens, that makes
the flower vanish on the stem
up high, as light
as the stems
of cherries,
like the cloud
pushed from the East,
like a blue branch
of rosewood in July.

A frontal flame, a flight
of smoke: lemon groves
in the winter under the volcanoes.

Come cavalli rovani
in corsa sul confine
di lunghe sabbie e di botri
va l'anima, attraversa
il regno del fuoco.

Like roan horses
running on the border
of long sands and ditches,
the soul goes, crossing
the kingdom of fire.

II

Dopo, passato anche il fuoco, ci sarà
soltanto la verità della luce.

La luce, lama, limite
che non si può raggiungere, ma che
gli occhi dell'uomo inseguono, finché
non sono più occhi.

Quando ci troveremo nel barbaglio
dove né dentro né fuori, né
mancina né destra, né
prima né poi esistono più
dove non ci saranno più inverno né
estate, calme foschie né
ghiacci viaggianti
là dove i punti
cardinali, quello di tramontana e
di libeccio e di scirocco
vorticano, si
fondono
in un solo punto, che specchia
stelle in una corolla di calendula

staremo allora nella luce, nella
verità
e ciascuno di noi conoscerà
il suo Dio.

II

Later, having even crossed the fire, there will only
be the truth of the light.

The light, blade, limit
that cannot be reached, but
that the eyes of men pursue
until they no longer are eyes.

When we will find ourselves in the glare
where neither inside nor outside
neither left nor right
neither before nor after will exist any longer,
where they will no longer be
neither winter nor summer, neither calm mists
nor traveling icebergs,
there where the cardinal points,
the one of the north wind,
of the southwest and of the south-east wind
whirl around,
fuse
in one point that reflects the stars
in the corolla of a calendula,

we will then be in the light,
in the truth
and each one of us will know
his God.

DOPO LE STAGIONI

AFTER THE SEASONS

I

Nella stagione in cui non fioriranno
né più si spoglieranno i ciliegi e i meli
vedremo le Città, passato il confine

su prati eterni di loto e di asfodeli.
Una città che a percorrerla quaranta
giorni di cammino occorreranno,

dalle mura di rame chiaro, le torri
. più lucenti dei fari, le piazze
più aperte dei deserti, e yucche

e euforbie e agavi nei giardini
sarà abitata dagli Angeli? Non so di
quale stirpe, se guerrieri

o sapienti, o come bambini
amanti del riso, del gioco.
Poi ne vedremo altre: città

dalle mura d'oro e di muschio, e di
fuoco, e sempre più percorse
da cavalli e da carovane.

Si dice che ci sono diecimila
giorni di strada da una porta all'altra
della Città capitale.

I

In the seasons when the cherry and the apple trees
will no longer blossom, no longer lose their leaves,
we shall see the Cities across the border

in eternal meadows of lotus and asphodels.
Will a city that takes forty
days to cross on foot,

a city with walls of bright copper, and towers
brighter than lighthouses, piazzas
more open than deserts, and yucca trees

and euphorbias and agaves in the gardens—
will it be inhabited by Angels? Of I-know-not-what-kind,
warriors or sages,

or like children,
loving laughter and play.
Then we shall see others: cities

with walls of gold, of moss, of
fire, crossed more and more
by horses and caravans.

They say it takes ten thousand days
to travel from one gate to the other
of the Capital city.

II

La città di Jâbarsâ sui confini[1]
occidentali, la città di Jâbalqâ, dove noi
pensiamo l'oriente, hanno le mura

di smeraldo, torrette per le scolte
e cupole come piccole
volte di mille cieli. Gli abitatori

non sanno chi fu Adamo, né le schiere,
le gerarchie degli Angeli hanno mai
incontrato, né in pace né in guerra.

E vanno per un prato di gigli e primule
per giardini di ibischi che non si chiudono
di oleandri che non temono i primi geli.

Oh, i frutti eterni, il miele, le sorgenti
di quelle due città: gli occhi mai vedono
il sole che si alza e il sole che cade;

i raggi che rischiarano, che
insegnano la strada sono quelli
sottili, inazzurrati dello smeraldo

delle mura. La luce è la verità.
La luce dura eterna. Sopra zattere
di luce viaggeremo sino a Jâbarsâ

e a Jâbalqâ, oltre il tramonto e oltre
l'alba, oltre ciò che fiorisce e che disfiora
oltre l'inverno e l'estate, la primavera

e l'autunno.

---

[1] *Jâbarsâ ... Jâbalqâ*: nomi delle città celesti nella mistica islamica. Cfr.: Henry Corbin, *Corps spirituel et Terre céleste: De l'Iran mazdéen à l'Iran shi'ite*, Paris, Buchet-Chastel, 1961.

II

The city of Jâbarsâ on the western[1]
border, the city of Jâbalqâ, where we
imagine the Orient, have walls

of emerald, turrets for sentries
and domes like the small vaults
of a thousand skies. The inhabitants

do not know who Adam was, nor have they
ever encountered the legions and the hierarchies
of Angels, neither in war nor in peace.

They walk through a meadow of lilies and primroses,
through gardens of hibiscus that do not close,
of oleanders that do not fear the first frosts.

Oh the eternal fruits, the honey, the springs
of those two cities: the eyes never see
the rising sun, the setting sun;

and the rays that give light, that show
the road are the subtle,
azured ones of the emerald

of the walls. Light is the truth.
Light lasts eternally. On rafts of
light we will travel as far as Jâbarsâ

and Jâbalqâ, beyond the sunset and beyond dawn,
beyond what blooms and what withers,
beyond winter and summer, spring

and autumn.

---

[1] The Cities of Jâbarsâ and Jâbalqâ: names of the celestial cities in Islamic Mysticism.
Cfr.: Henry Corbin, *Corps spirituel et Terre céleste: De l'Iran mazdéen à l'Iran shi'ite*,
Paris, Buchet-Chastel, 1961.

COMMIATO

In quale stagione ci rivedremo,
padre?

Avremo dimenticato tutto.
La tua sciarpa da ufficiale di picchetto
azzurro vivo, perduta
in chissà quale trasloco,
il tuo passo veloce, la tua voce
fiera, il tuo sorridere un poco
innocente e il tuo rabbuiarti
imperioso.

Niente resterà: né gli avori
che raccoglievi, né le rose
della casa di Baiardo, né le ortensie,
il tuo orgoglio,
né le corse in automobile che hai amato
sino a tardi,
né i miei libri, né i miei fogli.

Non lo vedremo arrivare
l'inverno con i suoi cristalli
sui rami dei susini e dei fichi
con l'oro scuro delle roverelle
non aspetteremo più i glicini
il celeste lunare della loro
fioritura sui rami di Corso
Inglesi e di via Hope[1]
non riavremo i campi
di stoppie, neri a precipizio
sotto la torre, tra i trapezi
verdi e lucidi, abbaglianti
degli aranceti
né le colline pesanti

---

[1] *Corso Inglesi e via Hope*: vie di Sanremo

ENVOI

In which season shall we meet again,
father?

We will have forgotten everything,
your orderly-officer's sash,
bright blue, lost
in who-knows-which move,
your swift step, your proud
voice, your smile a little
innocent and your imperious
frowning?

Nothing will remain: neither the ivory pieces
you collected, nor the roses
of the house in Baiardo, nor your prized hydrangeas,[1]
your pride,
nor the car races you loved
till a late age,
nor my books, nor my papers.

We will not see winter arrive
with its crystals
on the branches of the plum and the fig-trees
with the blue gold of the oak-trees,
we will no longer wait for the wistaria,
the lunar blue of their blossoms
on the branches leaning
on Corso Inglesi or Via Hope—[2]
we will not regain the fields of stubble
—black, falling headlong
under the tower, among the green
and shiny—dazzling
trapezes of the orange groves
nor the hills heavy with

---

[1] *Baiardo*: a small town of inland Liguria, where the Conte family used to have a country house.
[2] Corso Inglesi: or Via Hope: streets in Sanremo, Liguria.

di nebbie e bacche sopra Ceriana
e il sole che reclina
il capo come per le tante
vendemmie una vigna.

Ma ci ritroveremo dopo, dopo
le stagioni, dove l'amore è il sogno
fanno nascere ancora
come un figlio da un padre
da una Montagna un Fiume.
Su zattere di luce scenderemo
insieme vedremo rive
rocciose e rapide, canneti
di porpora, isole
invase dai colori dell'aurora. Viaggeremo
oltre ciò che fiorisce e disfiora
oltre il giorno e la sera
la primavera e l'autunno.

mists and berries above Ceriana
and the sun reclining
its head like a vineyard
for too many harvests.

But we will find each other afterwards, after
the seasons, where love and dream
generate still,
like a son from a father
from a Mountain a River.
On rafts of light we will descend
together, we will see rocky and rapid
banks, purple cane thickets,
islands invaded by the colors of dawn.
We will travel
beyond what blossoms and withers,
beyond the day and the night,
the spring and the fall.

AFTERWORD
by
MASSIMO MAGGIARI

Archetypal poetry will never perish. Still today, archetypal poetry roams the world with the power of a thousand voices, the power of ancestral forces, the power of myths. Archetypal poetry has what Lorca called *duende* and connects life with death. It makes the heart pound, sharpens our senses and evokes in our hearts a sense of mystery and awe. Where does archetypal poetry take us? In a world plagued with literalism, where trees are trees and rocks are rocks, archetypal poetry make us embark on a journey to faraway lands where we visit primordial oceans, Achaean altars, emerald groves, reincarnations, re-flowerings, unknown cities and crossings presided by angels or *daimones*. There, at last, we plunge into the abysmal and magmatic pit of our origins, in the distant time of our ancestors. This is the only place and time when the Muses come and still bestow inspiration on the poets. At this crossroad where imagination and soul meet, we can experience a poetic initiation and recover a broader perception of life and Cosmos. Archetypal poetry is living the poetry of the world.

I have walked along Giuseppe Conte's path for some time now. I recognize his words as familiar and insightful. I share his vision of myth. I admire his poetry. His poetic journey includes all the stages of ancient initiation and calls for a transcendence from the constraints of the ego ("But later, at the climax of the air, the soul "), a connection with death ("Hades"), and an inner transformation ("Later, having even crossed the fire, there will only"). But, above all, I admire Conte's poetry because it is one of the most exhilarating and transporting vehicles my imagination could find to travel. It is effective and penetrating. It does not evolve, rather it always circles around an image to make a new vision prevail. Giuseppe Conte's poetry captures with a keen eye the archetypal halo of things. It recognizes the different field of energies where gods and goddesses preside with trans-empirical importance. Thus his poetic images influence the soul's imagination by broadening the events of nature from concrete details to aesthetic imagistic universals. The poetic landscape becomes a mythical field of personifications: *I will belong to no one. I will remain / mistress of the steep woods,/ of pine and poplars / trembling in the nights and the moons./ I will send hinds to run / till the very ends of the paths.* ("Artemis"). Images become animated and pervaded by an intentional force that offers an instinctive direction for destiny: *I ask myself: What is my soul?/ What ways does it have?/ ... / You know the ways of the souls./ And I know you: you are Hermes* ("I ask myself"). A greater love is embraced, a passionate love that can extend beyond oneself to include the world and its soul-fullness: *Love is / recognizing oneself in everything, in the first / rose of the world / in the last / ranunculus, in the low tide, in the deep / ocean* ("The lover").

We also thank Laura Stortoni-Hager for making this Italian poet accessible to the English-speaking world. Her translations respect the original texts and have an effect that captivates, charms and quickens our readership. I believe that, thanks to initiatives like this, poetry still matters today.

BIBLIOGRAPHY
Works by Giuseppe Conte

POETRY
Il processo di comunicazione secondo Sade. Napoli: Altri termini,1975.
L'ultimo aprile bianco. Milano: Società di poesia, 1979.
Un chant pour des résurrections songées. Trans. J. P. Faye, in *Change*, 39, 1980.
Il mare degli anemoni, in *Almanacco dello specchio*, no. 10. Milano: Mondadori, 1981.
L'Oceano e il Ragazzo. Milano: Rizzoli, 1983.
Le stagioni. Milano: Rizzoli, 1988.
Dialogo del poeta e del messaggero. Milano: Mondadori, 1992.
Canti d'oriente e d'occidente. Milano: Mondadori, 1997.

ANTHOLOGIES AND WORKS OF CRITICISM
La metafora. Milano: Feltrinelli, 1981.
La lirica d'occidente. Milano: Guanda, 1990.
La poesia nel mondo. Milano: Guanda, 2001.

FICTION/TRAVEL
Primavera incendiata. Milano: Feltrinelli, 1980.
Equinozio d'autunno. Milano: Rizzoli, 1987.
Le manuscript de Saint-Nazaire. MEET, 1989 (dual-language edition).
I giorni della nuvola. Milano: Rizzoli, 1990.
Terre del mito. Milano: Mondadori, 1991.
Fedeli d'amore. Milano: Rizzoli, 1993.
L'impero e l'incanto. Milano: Rizzoli, 1995.
Il ragazzo che parla col sole. Milano: Longanesi, 1998. (Pocket edition: Tea, 1999.)
Il terzo ufficiale. Milano: Longanesi, 2001.

THEATER
Boine. Two acts for music, in collaboration with Gianni Possio. Milano: Rugginenti. 1986.
Veglia. Chamber oratorio for soloists, chorus and orchestra sextet based on an idea of Mimmo Paladino. Pescara: Carsa Edizioni, 1992.
Re Artù e i senzatetto / Le Roy Arthur et les sans-logis. MEET (dual-language edition), 1995.
Ungaretti fa l'amore. Quaderni dell'Ariston, Sanremo, 2000.

TRANSLATIONS BY GIUSEPPE CONTE
Shelley, Percy Bysshe. "Ode al vento di ponente." *Il Verri* 12 (1978).
Lawrence, D. H. *La donna che fuggì a cavallo*. Milano: Guanda, 1980.
Blake, William. "Canti dell'innocenza" and "Canti dell'esperienza." *Opere*. Milano: Guanda, 1984.

Lawrence, D. H. *Poesie.* Milano: Mondadori, 1987.
Shelley, Percy Bysshe. *Poesie.* Milano: Rizzoli, 1989.
Whitman, Walt. *Foglie d'erba.* Milano: Mondadori. 1991.

CRITICISM
La metafora barocca. Milano: Mursia, 1972.
La metafora. Milano: Feltrinelli, 1981.
"*Retorica e logica nell'estetica barocca.*" In *Sigma*, no. 25, 1970.
"La neve nel gelato di fragole. Il segno del giorno." *Altri termini* 2 (1972).
"Passioni e istituzioni nell'estetica del Settecento." *Studi di estetica* 2 (1974/75).
"D. H. Lawrence". *Il Verri* 17 (1980).
Sulla poesia. Conversazioni nelle scuole (with Bertolucci, Sereni, Zanzotto, Porta, Cucchi). Parma: Pratiche, 1989.
Il mito giardino. Siracusa, Sicily: Edizioni di Tema celeste, 1990.
Manuale di poesia. Milano: Guanda, 1995.
Il sonno degli dei. Milano: Rizzoli, 1999.
Il passaggio di Ermes. Milano: Ponte delle Grazie, 1999.

TRANSLATIONS OF GIUSEPPE CONTE
L'Océan et l'Enfant. Trans. Jean-Baptiste Para. Paris : Arcane 17, 1989.
Les saisons. Trans. Jean-Baptiste Para. N. P. Cahier de Royaumont, 1989.
Osennee Ravnogenstvie (Equinozio d'autunno). Moscow : Raduga, 1993.
Terres du mythe. Trans. Nathalie Campodonico. Paris : Arcane 17, 1993.
The Ocean and The Boy. Trans. and ed. Laura Stortoni. Berkeley: Hesperia Press, 1997.

SELECTED ARTICLES ON GIUSEPPE CONTE

INTRODUCTION TO POETRY COLLECTIONS
Ficara, Giorgio. "Introduzione a G. Conte." *L'Oceano e il ragazzo.* Milano: Rizzoli, 1983. 5-16.
_____. "Introduzione a G. Conte." *Le stagioni.* Milano: Rizzoli, 1988. 5-16.

NEWSPAPER, MAGAZINE, AND JOURNAL ARTICLES
Anceschi, Luciano. "Variazione su alcuni equilibri della poesia che san di essere precari." *Il Verri* 1 (1976): 5-20.
Barbolini, R. "Cavallette in rima." *Panorama* (Oct. 30, 1988).
Barilli, R. "Altre letture." *L'Espresso* (Nov. 18, 1979).
Baudino, Mario. "Ecco cosa sa un poeta." *Stampa sera* (Dec. 10, 1983).
_____. "Quel gabbiano è un dio." *Stampa sera* (Nov. 7, 1988).
Bertolucci, Attilo. "Sarà nella tempesta." *Panorama* (Apr. 5, 1987).
Bo, Carlo. "Ma dove va la poesia?" *Corriere della sera* (Mar. 11, 1987).

_____. "Nei versi di Giuseppe Conte riecheggia il primo D'Annunzio." *Corriere della sera*, Oct. 30, 1988.

Calvino, Italo. "Un poeta per Diana." *La repubblica* (Jan. 12, 1984).

Cancogni, M. "Il poeta è un'arma tagliente." *Il giornale* (Oct. 5, 1985).

Carifi, Roberto. "Aspetti teorico-critici della 'nuova poesia.'" *Nuova corrente, poesia per gli anni 80 (II)*, 89 (1982): 508-33.

_____. *Il gesto di Callicle. Saggio sulla nuova poesia.* Milano: Società di poesia, 1982.

_____. "Il ragazzo che interroga l'oceano." *I quaderni del battello ebbro* 6-7 (Dec. 1990): 19-22.

_____. "Giuseppe Conte. Il mito e la poesia." In Introduction to *Anni '80. Poesia italiana.* Ed. L. Cesari. Milano: Jaca Book, 1993. 7-13.

Citati, Pietro. "Cacciatore di simboli." *Corriere della sera* (Mar. 7, 1987).

_____. "Quando gli dei inventarono la poesia." *La repubblica* (Dec. 11, 1990).

_____. "Le scarpe metafisiche." *La repubblica* (Mar. 12, 1992).

Copioli, Rosita. "Sopravvivere con il gatto." *Il giornale* (July 1, 1990).

_____. "Movimenti di natura e anima in *Equinozio d'autunno.*" *I quaderni del battello ebbro* 6-7 (Dec. 1990): 23-29.

Crespi, S. "Isole e canneti invasi dai colori dell'aurora." *Sole 24 Ore*, (Dec. 4, 1988).

De Angelis, G. *Il canto ritrovato. D'Annunzio e i poeti contemporanei.* Edizioni Tracce, 1995. 17-23.

De Angelis, Milo. "Per Giuseppe Conte." *I quaderni del battello ebbro* 6-7 (Dec. 1990): 30-31.

De Nicola, F. "I poeti sono tra noi." In *Il lavoro*, Dec. 18, 1984.

_____. "Giuseppe Conte." *Il mare. Avventura e mito.* *Nove scrittori per un'idea di Liguria.* Genova: N.P., 1989. 127-29.

Di Mauro, Antonio. "Viaggio al punto del non ritorno. Una nuova 'stagione' nella poesia di Giuseppe Conte." *Si scrive*, only edition, 1995. 392-95.

Faggi, V. "Tutte le nostre stagioni." *Il secolo XIX* (Jan. 25, 1989).

Ferullo, E. "Giuseppe Conte: dialogo d'un poeta con la propria anima." *Pelagos* (July 3, 1996): 51-65.

Ficara, Giorgio. "In un territorio mitico." *Alfabeta* 97 (June 1987).

_____. "Sublime apocalisse." *Panorama* (Apr. 8, 1990).

Forti, Marco. Introduction, *Il mare degli anemoni. Almanacco dello specchio* 10 (1981): 271-73.

_____. "Giuseppe Conte: mito metamorfosi e deità in esilio." *Lunario nuovo* 28:6 (Jan.-Feb. 1984): 33-42.

Guglielmi, Angelo. "Conte, viva il sole dopo l'apocalisse." *Tuttolibri, La stampa* (May 19, 1990).

Kemeny, Tomaso. "Nomi della poesia contemporanea e altre domande." *Autografo* 1 (1984): 20-31.

Kemeny, Tomaso, and C. Viviani,, eds. *I percorsi della nuova poesia italiana.* Napoli: Guida Editori, 1980.

Lecchini, S. "Una voce dalle stelle." *Cultura, Gazzetta di Parma* (Apr. 5, 1995).

Marchetti, Giuseppe. "Ma si impara il mestiere di poeta?" *Cultura, Gazzetta di Parma* (Apr. 5, 1995).

Martini, D.G. "Natura e mito, i fulcri della poesia di Conte." *Il giornale* (Feb. 1, 1989).

Maugeri, A. "Il colore della voce." *Corriere del Ticino* (Mar. 11, 1989).

Meda, Anna. "Visione e mito in *Le stagioni* di Giuseppe Conte." *I quaderni del battello ebbro* 6-7 (Dec. 1990): 32-38.

Mezzalama, C. "Poesia come custode della bellezza." *Erba d'Arno* 64-65 (Spring-Summer, 1996).

Mondo, L. "Le leggende celtiche fioriscono sul mare di Liguria." *Tuttolibri, La stampa* (Mar. 14, 1987).

Montefoschi, G. "Il mantello di Flora." *Il messaggero* (Dec. 3, 1988).

Moriconi, A. M. "Dei e miti vivono ancora nella natura." *Il mattino* (Dec. 6, 1988).

Mussapi, "Il poeta della felicità." *Elle* 12 (Dec. 1988).

_____. "Canta la natura il poeta Conte." *Il giornale* (Dec. 24, 1988).

Ombres, R. "La natura danza sull'oceano." *Tuttolibri, La stampa* (Jan. 21, 1984).

Pampaloni, G. "I 'misteri' della scrittura." *Il giornale* (Mar. 8, 1987).

Paolini, Alcide. "Una poesia che non teme il tono alto." *Corriere della sera* (Sept. 5, 1984).

Paris, R. "È nato il romanzo 'verde'?" *Paese sera* (Mar. 22, 1987).

Pinson, Jean-Claude. "*L'Oceano e il Ragazzo*, trad. M. Teodori." *I quaderni del battello ebbro* 6-7 (Dec. 1990): 39-40.

Porta, A. "*Quattro poeti per una nuova collana.*" *Corriere della sera* (July 29, 1979).

Portinari, F. "Questo poeta riscopre la mitologia." *Tuttolibri, La stampa* (Jan. 28, 1989).

Stefanelli, E. "Le stagioni del mito." *La Sicilia* (Dec. 4, 1988).

Testa, E. "Il codice imperfetto della 'nuova poesia.'" *Nuova corrente, poesia per gli anni 80 (II)*, 89 (1982): 535-84.

Vetri, L. "Riduzione, dispersione, disseminazione dell'io [1]." *Il Verri* 20-21 (1980/1).

Vicentini, I. "È aria nuova nelle 'Stagioni' di Conte." *Il tempo* (Nov.18, 1988).

Vitali, C. "Giuseppe Conte: un nuovo romanticismo?" *La vanguardia* (Sep. 30, 1986).

Zagarrio, G. *Febbre, furore e fiele. Repertorio della poesia italiana contemporanea 1970-1980.* Milano: Mursia, 1983.

Zecchi, Stefano. "Ermes padre dei poeti." *Il giornale* (Dec. 16, 1990).

ABOUT THE EDITOR-TRANSLATOR

Laura Stortoni-Hager was born in Italy and educated in Europe. She has received higher education degrees in Comparative Literature at the University of California, Berkeley. She has published her own poetry and poetry translation in several major magazines and journals.

She specializes in Italian Women Renaissance poetry, and has edited and co-translated, with Mary Prentice Lillie, *Gaspara Stampa: Selected Poems* (New York: Italica Press, 1994) and an anthology, *Women Poets of the Italian Renaissance: Courtly Ladies and Courtesans* (New York: Italica Press, 1997).

Laura Stortoni-Hager has also edited and translated a dual-language edition of Maria Luisa Spaziani's *Sentry Towers* (Berkeley: Hesperia Press, 1997), as well as Giuseppe Conte's *The Ocean and the Boy*, also in dual-language edition, with an introduction by Italo Calvino (Berkeley: Hesperia Press, 1997). She has authored the *The Moon and the Island*, a volume of her personal poetry with an introduction by Diane di Prima. She is presently working on two Renaissance Italian women writers, Isabella Andreini and Sara Copio Sullam, in preparation for two volumes for the University of Chicago Press. She has recently completed two volumes of personal poetry in her native Italian, *Ti riprendo* and *Il ritorno*.

Laura Stortoni-Hager makes her home in Berkeley, California, and Milano, Italy.